STUDENT SKILLS

TUTOR'S HANDBOOK

STUDENT SKILLS

TUTOR'S HANDBOOK

SUE DREW

and

ROSIE BINGHAM

Learning and Teaching Institute

Sheffield Hallam University

Gower

Details of a photocopy licence, and other Student Skills materials, are given at the back of this book.

Published by
Gower Publishing Limited
Gower House
Croft Road
Aldershot
Hampshire GU11 3HR
England

Gower
Old Post Road
Brookfield
Vermont 05036
USA

Reprinted 1997

Sue Drew, Rosie Bingham, Theresa Lillis, Andrew Walker and Aileen Wade have asserted their right under the Copyright, Designs and Patents Act 1988 to be identified as the authors of this work.

The Student Skills Tutor's Handbook was edited by Sue Drew and Rosie Bingham.

British Library Cataloguing in Publication Data.
A catalogue record for this book is available from the British Library.

ISBN   0 566 07846 5

Typeset in England by Neil Straker Creative
and printed in Great Britain by MPG Books Ltd, Bodmin, Cornwall

CONTENTS

THE AUTHORS OF THE SKILLPACKS

Identifying Strengths and Improving Skills
  Sue Drew and Rosie Bingham

Organising Yourself and Your Time
  Sue Drew and Rosie Bingham

Note Taking
  Sue Drew and Rosie Bingham

Gathering and Using Information
  Sue Drew, Aileen Wade and Andrew Walker

Essay Writing
  Theresa Lillis

Report Writing
  Sue Drew and Rosie Bingham

Oral Presentation
  Sue Drew and Rosie Bingham

Solving Problems
  Sue Drew and Rosie Bingham

Group Work
  Sue Drew and Rosie Bingham

Negotiating and Assertiveness
  Sue Drew and Rosie Bingham

Coping with Pressure
  Sue Drew and Rosie Bingham

Revising and Examination Techniques
  Sue Drew and Rosie Bingham

ABOUT THE AUTHORS

Sue Drew is a Senior Lecturer at Sheffield Hallam University. She has worked there since 1975, before which she was in industry doing personnel work. She was a careers adviser until 1987, when with a colleague she initiated the Personal Skills and Qualities Project. She is now part of the Learning and Teaching Institute, which provides support for curriculum development and educational research for the University. In 1993, she became responsible for a project funded by TEED (now the Department for Education and Employment), to develop and trial the series of student SkillPacks which now form the basis for this book.

Rosie Bingham has many years experience teaching in primary schools in Sheffield and in Teacher Training for the School of Education at Sheffield Hallam University. She has been working in the Learning and Teaching Institute of the University since 1993 and has been involved in all aspects of the SkillPacks project, but particularly with the trialling and evaluation of the materials.

Theresa Lillis taught for ten years in a Sheffield secondary school where she held specific responsibilities for the language development of both first and second language speakers of English. In recent years she has been involved in adult basic education, as well as teaching on a range of courses in education and linguistics at higher education level. She is currently based at the Learning and Teaching Institute carrying out research with a group of mature women students into their experience of writing at university.

Aileen Wade has worked as a computing, engineering and science information specialist at Sheffield Hallam University for more than 16 years. She has extensive experience of training library users in how to exploit electronic information resources. She is active in promoting higher education and research communities' network (JANET) and has represented her profession at a national level for many years.

Andrew Walker has provided business and computing information to industry and HE for over 10 years. He is currently the Business Information Specialist at Sheffield Hallam University. Previously he has been a Business Analyst to Binder Hamlyn, and an Information Specialist and Systems Analyst to Coopers Lybrand Deloitte.

ACKNOWLEDGEMENTS

The materials in this book were the result of collaborative work with colleagues. In particular, we would like to thank Roger Payne of Sheffield Hallam University whose original idea it was to develop the SkillPacks.

The SkillPacks Steering Group

- Roger Harrison – Open University
- Peter Hartley – Sheffield Hallam University
- Ranald Macdonald – Sheffield Hallam University
- Sue Morton – Sheffield Hallam University
- David Pierce – TEED, now the Department for Education and Employment
- Jane Whalen and Chris Buck – Union of Students, Sheffield Hallam University

The Steering Group members gave invaluable advice and guidance on the content, format and use of the materials.

Sheffield Hallam University staff and students

We would like to thank all those staff and students who generously agreed to have their teaching sessions observed, to provide class time for student consultations or who distributed questionnaires, and also those who gave considerable time to provide suggestions and feedback:

- Sheffield Hallam University students
- Staff of the Learning and Teaching Institute (LTI), Sheffield Hallam University
- Many staff from Schools and Departments within Sheffield Hallam University, but particularly –
  - Mary Burgess
  - Sharon Clancy
  - Dave Hurry
  - Pat Quinn
  - Linda Purdy
  - Diane Rushton
  - Aileen Wade

Thanks are due to the following Sheffield Hallam University tutors who gave permission for us to use examples of their work in Section 1.7:

- Richard Crampton – School of Engineering
- Hilary Cunliffe-Charlesworth – School of Cultural Studies
- Dave Hurry – School of Cultural Studies
- Dave Parsons – School of Urban and Regional Studies
- Diane Rushton – School of Leisure and Food Management
- SITCOM team, via Jennie Shelton – School of Science

- Amanda Smith – School of Urban and Regional Studies
- Christine Straker – School of Computing and Management Sciences
- Des Wilson – School of Education

Thanks also to Melanie Ramsey of The Sheffield College.

Production support

We would like to acknowledge the contribution, in the form of their support in the production of the materials, of the following:
- Ian Lawrence
- Andy Pettigrew
- Mark Pettigrew
- Pamela Powell
- June Wragg
- Geoff Wilkinson

Finally, thanks to the following people who provided valuable advice on the first chapter of this Handbook:
- John Arnold – Manchester School of Management
- Professor Asher Cashdan – LTI, Sheffield Hallam University
- Maggie Challis – LTI, Sheffield Hallam University
- Peter Hartley – School of Cultural Studies, Sheffield Hallam University
- Mark Neath – LTI, Sheffield Hallam University

1
HOW TO USE THIS BOOK

by Sue Drew and Rosie Bingham

CONTENTS

The materials in this book were developed in response to a specific request by engineering degree course staff for materials which could help them run a personal and professional development unit (module). They felt that their expertise lay more in the teaching of their subject but also recognised the importance of a wide range of skills which can be seen as generally relevant across disciplines.

The Training Enterprise and Education Directorate (TEED) of the Employment Department (now the Department for Education and Employment) agreed to fund a project over 1993–94 to identify further topics and to develop materials which would be appropriate across subject areas. Through the project a series of student SkillPacks were drafted, piloted and amended to create the chapters of this book.

The pilot of the materials was very extensive. Over 2000 students from different disciplines and levels/years at Sheffield Hallam University were involved, as were academic staff. An evaluator observed class sessions where the materials were used, ran structured group sessions with students to find out their views, and gathered further information from a questionnaire. The drafts were then amended in the light of student and staff views about what was helpful. During the first year of usage of the final materials over 25 000 copies were used within Sheffield Hallam University, and during the second year over 47 000 copies were used.

1.1 WHY SKILLS ARE IMPORTANT

1.1.1 Academic skills

It has always been recognised in higher education that, in order to cope with academic work, students need to develop a wide range of skills and personal qualities. Such attributes help students to acquire and use knowledge and also to communicate their knowledge and understanding to assessors. They include:

- **being able to locate and use information**
- **cognitive skills such as the ability to make connections or to analyse**
- **being able to deal with lecturers and other students effectively**
- **being able to write or talk about their subject**
- **becoming independent.**

There is, however, an increasing focus on such attributes, and there are a number of reasons for this.

- **The pace of change** means that knowledge may quickly become outdated and implies that individuals need to be able to learn and update their knowledge continually. This has led to a greater focus on the skills needed for "lifelong learning".

- **The move towards mass higher education** has meant increased student numbers with no increase in resources or with reduced resources. One response has been to consider how to encourage students to be more autonomous in their learning, and this implies that greater attention should be given to the skills they need for this.

- **Mass higher education** also means a different student body. It is no longer possible to assume that all new students will be 18 and with an A level background. Students now come from more varied backgrounds and with more varied experience; they have differing motivations and existing levels of academic skill. This suggests a need to concentrate more specifically on those academic skills necessary for success.

- **Increased emphasis** is now placed on the process of learning, as well as on subject content. Students' abilities to handle that process are dependent on the use of a range of skills which can improve a student's grasp of the subject. Kolb (1984), for example, has offered a model of experiential learning which involves having an experience, and then reflecting upon it in order to form generalisations which can then be used for a new experience. Experiential learning methods, such as project work or group activities, tend to involve a wider use of skills than the more traditional didactic methods.

Higher education has always claimed to develop a wide range of attributes in students. For example, the Council for National Academic Awards, established in 1964, had as part of its aims:

... the development of students' intellectual and imaginative powers; their understanding and judgement; their problem solving skills; their ability to communicate; their ability to see relationships within what they have learned and to perceive their field of study in a broader perspective. Each student's programme of study must stimulate an enquiring, analytical and creative approach, encouraging independent judgement and critical self awareness. (CNAA 1989)

However, the attributes developed in students have often been implicit rather than explicit. For some time research has indicated that students give most attention to that which is assessed (see, for example, Becker *et al*, 1968). Traditional assessment has focused on subject content and, whilst students' personal attributes – for example their communication skills – have influenced their grades, this may not have been acknowledged via assessment criteria. Students may therefore be unaware of the importance of such attributes or may develop them without being aware of them and consequently find it difficult to articulate exactly what skills they have acquired through their courses. This relates to the second principal reason for an increased emphasis on skills.

1.1.2 Skills for employment

The increased fluidity of the employment market and rapid technological change has led to a growing emphasis on employees' abilities to adapt to new situations. This in turn has brought about a focus on what are usually termed "transferable skills" – a term which is generally used to describe those skills which are important across most employment areas, rather than those which are specific to particular professions, such as design or laboratory skills.

Both employers, through such organisations as the Confederation of British Industry (CBI), and government have complained that students are inadequately prepared for the world of work. The Association of Graduate Recruiters (1993) has emphasised the importance employers attach to personal attributes and indicates that employers select graduates from similar institutions on the basis of such attributes. The CBI (1989) and the Trades Union Congress (1989) have both endorsed the view that education must develop in individuals a range of skills which will enable them to adapt flexibly to the changing world of employment. Throughout the 1980s there emerged a plethora of government papers and initiatives focusing on the development of such "transferable skills" in students – for example *A New Training Initiative* (MSC, 1981), *Better Schools* (DES, 1985), *Working Together – Education and Training* (DES, 1986), *The Development of Higher Education into the 1990s* (DES, 1985), *Higher Education – Meeting the Challenge* (DES, 1987).

Employers stress that employees must be able to communicate well both in writing and verbally, and to deal with others effectively. Employment structures tend increasingly to be less hierarchical and more team-oriented which implies that employees should be able to solve problems, acquire new knowledge and be flexible. The CBI (1989) has referred to values and integrity, effective communication, application of numeracy, application of technology, understanding of the world of work and the world, personal and interpersonal skills, problem solving and positive attitudes to change. The following quotations are from 1995–96 graduate recruitment literature.

As you would be working closely with both clients and colleagues in a variety of disciplines, you will need mature social skills and must be able to communicate lucidly and persuasively, both orally and in writing. (Ove Arup – Civil Engineering)

Personal qualities are as important to us as academic qualifications. We look for the following in all our recruits: drive and enthusiasm; problem solving skills and thoroughness; interpersonal and communication skills; leadership qualities and vision. (British Steel)

It may be partly because students find it so difficult to articulate the skills they have acquired from their education, and to relate them to work, that employers have gained the impression that such skills are poorly developed. There has therefore been an increasing focus not only on making such skills more explicit but also on providing a wider range of learning experiences, so that students are able to practise the skills required at work. This has led to educational approaches such as group work, the use of realistic case studies, simulations of work situations through activities such as project work, or the use of learning contracts to encourage autonomy in students. It has also led to new assessment methods, since lecturers have begun to use the motivational power of assessment to encourage students to take seriously such skills as, for example, giving oral presentations.

1.2 ARE SKILLS TRANSFERABLE?

In the literature on skills development in higher education (eg National Advisory Body, 1986) there is an assumption that those skills which are generally applicable to educational and employment settings are automatically transferable. However, there is little research to support this view (Oates, 1992a). Students who have developed the ability to argue a case in a seminar group may find it difficult to link this activity with a similar one in a work setting.

There is some evidence to indicate that, in order for an individual to transfer a skill from one situation to another, he or she must be able to recognise the connections between the two situations, assess the new situation and identify what would be appropriate behaviour. Schon (1987) refers to "reflection in action" – the ability to see what is appropriate at the time. Skills should be made explicit to students to help them become more aware of what they are doing, and the context in which they practise these skills should be similar to the context in which they will subsequently have to use them. It follows that course tasks should relate to "real world" tasks and that students need a way of thinking about skills. They need to develop cognitive skills which enable them to evaluate situations, reflect on their behaviour and identify appropriate behaviours for a particular context. Attitudes may be crucial. For example, students may be more likely to amend their behaviour in a group if they acknowledge that their actions influence what others do, than if they believe that effective group work depends solely on chance or on who is in the group.

The implications for teaching are as follows:

- Skills are best developed alongside subject knowledge rather than separately, so that students can recognise the context in which they will be used.

- Skills development must be made explicit and be seen to be valued – for example through assessment.

- Students should be encouraged to become aware of their **own** usage of skills and to identify what will work for them in a given situation, rather than be given a ready-made tool kit. Self-assessment can be helpful here.

- Students should reflect on their actions and identify what might be appropriate for a given context; they need to progress from being guided to becoming more autonomous in their use of skills.

1.3 CORE SKILLS

A significant recent impact on education and training in general has been the establishment of the National Council for Vocational Qualifications. NCVQ has developed a framework for National Vocational Qualifications (NVQs) to rationalise vocational training. There are five levels of NVQ, of which level 3 has been mapped against the "A" level, level 4 against final-year degree level (but not the exit graduation point), and level 5 against postgraduate or professional level.

Following an initial identification of possible core skills for 16–19 year olds by the National Curriculum Council (NCC, 1990), NCVQ and the Schools Examination and Assessment Council (SEAC) were asked by the government to develop a set of core skills in NVQs and A/AS levels respectively. NCVQ did most of the subsequent development work on core skills, building on the work of the NCC, the CBI, and a variety of education and training bodies such as BTEC to develop a framework of six core skills which they see as relevant to all educational and work contexts (Oates, 1992b).

Core skills are intended to be relevant to a range of qualifications. They have been embedded in the new General National Vocational Qualifications (GNVQ) which are currently being taught in schools and further education colleges. Three of the core skills are obligatory parts of a GNVQ. In addition, BTEC, the Royal Society of Arts (RSA) and City and Guilds (C&G) certificates each core skill as a separate unit. Core skills can now form part of NVQs, and there have been discussions about their place in the school curriculum and in higher education. This core skills framework is likely to become increasingly influential in the educational world.

Core Skill	Status	
Communication	Obligatory in GNVQs	
Information technology		
Application of number		Can form part of NVQs Units can be accredited by BTEC, RSA and C&G
Personal skills – working with others	Optional in GNVQs	
Personal skills – improving own learning and performance		
Problem solving	NCVQ has produced specifications but has not accredited this as one of its core skills. BTEC, RSA, and C&G, however, certificate a core skill unit in this area	

The topics covered in this book can be seen to be relevant to four of the above skill areas. Materials are currently being developed by Sheffield Hallam University on the other two: application of number and information technology.

Core skill	Topics included in this book
Personal skills – improving own learning and performance	Identifying Strengths and Improving Skills Organising Yourself and Your Time Coping with Pressure Revising and Examination Techniques
Communication	Note Taking Gathering and Using Information Essay Writing Report Writing Oral Presentation
Personal skills – dealing with others	Group Work Negotiating and Assertiveness
Problem solving	Solving Problems

1.4 ABOUT THE MATERIALS IN THIS BOOK

1.4.1 The SkillPacks

The materials in this book were originally produced as individual SkillPacks for students. They now each form a chapter in this book. Each SkillPack title includes references and a bibliography. These are also gathered together at the end of this book, for greater convenience.

Gower also publish the following:

- *The Student Skills Guide*
  This is a paperback for students, which includes all the SkillPacks and an introduction about how best to use them.

- *SkillPack Booklets*
  These are printed sets of the SkillPack booklets, available to tutors. Each title can be separately purchased in multiples of 10.

- *Student Skills: SkillPack Masters*
  This is a set of originals of the SkillPacks which can be photocopied, for use with students.

Full details of these related products are provided at the end of this book in the section *Student Skills Product List* (see contents).

1.4.2 The level of the SkillPacks

The pilot at Sheffield Hallam University, referred to earlier, established that students' responses to the materials partly depended on their perception of their current skill level. Skill development can be seen to be progressive, with individuals achieving increasing levels of a skill. When amended, the materials were therefore produced at two levels. In order to do this, learning outcomes were drafted for each level and the SkillPacks were based on those outcomes. These two levels were based upon the NCVQ core skill specifications at their levels 3 (our Starter level) and 4 (our Development level) although they are not identical to them. The relevant learning outcomes are given at the end of this chapter.

The SkillPacks in this book are divided into two Parts:

Part I: Starter level

Part I contains SkillPacks designed for students with little existing expertise in the area. Materials in this Part could also be useful for students who feel they can already handle a topic to remind them of things they may have forgotten or to give a fresh slant on the issues.

Part II: Development level

Part II contains SkillPacks on the same topics but at a more advanced level. Materials in this Part assume that students have some existing expertise, and build on the SkillPacks in Part I. The SkillPacks cover the same topics as Part I, apart from "Note Taking", which is at Starter level only.

1.4.3 The underlying principles in the design of the SkillPacks

Relevance

The pilot established that it was very important for students to see the immediate relevance of the materials. The materials have, therefore, been written so that each pack can be used in conjunction with a course activity. For example, the starting point for the SkillPack on "Group Work" is that the student is operating in a group for a particular purpose, and that for "Report Writing" is that s/he must produce a report.

Awareness raising

The materials aim to raise students' awareness of how they approach a skill. They therefore try to avoid being prescriptive and do not suggest that there is a single right way to do something unless there is a commonly used method. For example, although there is no absolute standard in referencing work, we have suggested the Harvard system as it is probably the most widely adopted. The Packs: offer a range of suggestions, ask the students to consider what might work best for them, and invite them to review progress and plan any actions they need to take to improve their skill level.

A "deep" approach

Marton and Saljo (1984) found that students tend to take particular approaches to learning tasks and that this determines what they actually do. Students taking a surface approach perceive the learning task to be about acquiring factual information, and those taking a deep approach perceive that they should look for underlying concepts. A deep approach is more helpful for "lifelong learning". The same student may take either approach in different circumstances. Surface approaches are encouraged by a heavy workload and having to cover a lot of material, by authoritarian and anxiety-provoking contexts, and by assessment which encourages them to reproduce factual information. Deep approaches are encouraged by having more time to study the material, by less authoritarian and more supportive contexts, and by assessment tasks which encourage an emphasis on understanding and on concepts. The SkillPacks aim to promote a deep approach to students' skill development, by encouraging them to think about what they are doing and why, rather than just giving a series of instructions and handy hints.

Interaction

The materials are interactive and contain exercises for the students to complete, which aim to take them further with their particular task. The trial made it clear that, if students were to use them, the self-completion boxes had to have a very clear purpose and be seen to move the individual on.

Appearance

The appearance and length of the materials were important factors. The amended versions are as concise as possible, the layout has been improved, and for student use they are each printed in a different colour (this seems a minor consideration but it was actually very important to the students, as it made them stand out in their files).

1.5 USING THE SKILLPACKS

1.5.1 As open learning materials/for class activities

Staff find themselves under continual and increasing pressure. Modularisation, semesterisation and increased student numbers have all meant increased pressure on class contact time in which to deliver both subject content and skills. Whilst academic staff may feel very confident in their subject area, they may feel less so in supporting students' skill development. The materials in this book were therefore designed to support lecturers who would be unable to find the time to prepare such materials themselves. They can be used in two main ways: as open learning materials by students, thereby relieving pressure on class time, and also as a whole or in part within class activities – their clear sections lend themselves very well to this.

1.5.2 Key factors for lecturers and tutors to consider

The trial established a number of important factors concerning how the materials are best used with students.

Usage across disciplines

The materials can be effectively used across a range of disciplines. For some topics lecturers or tutors might also provide subject-specific examples – eg for "Report Writing" an example of a report in a format acceptable to the discipline is helpful.

Relevance and timing

Students are most likely to find the materials useful if they are given in conjunction with a relevant course activity and at an appropriate time. It is more effective to distribute the SkillPacks as and when a particular task requires that skill than to provide them as a reference set at the start of a course. "Report Writing" can therefore be given out at the same time as an assignment brief requiring a report, or "Group Work" can be distributed when the students are required to form a project group. This encourages students to see their relevance.

Motivation

Students are more likely to be motivated to use a SkillPack if:

• it is introduced by a lecturer, albeit briefly, as this gives credibility to the topic

- it is discussed or used in some way in class, if there is time (some lecturers have used sections of the materials as they stand or amended them, giving examples from their own subject, for class activities)

- it is placed in the context of the subject and related to a learning task

- the skill appears as part of the assessment criteria for a piece of work. Section 1.6 below deals specifically with the important issue of assessment.

Coordination

There are logistical difficulties associated with using the materials in conjunction with specific tasks, especially on modularised courses. How can coordination be achieved so that SkillPacks are not duplicated between units or modules or that coverage of the appropriate skills is assured? How can progression be ensured so that students continue to develop skills in subsequent years of their courses?

The answer to these questions will depend on the particular institution but, at Sheffield Hallam University, the problem has been addressed in a variety of ways.

- There are unitised programmes each with a programme leader. This person has taken on responsibility for coordinating the usage of the SkillPacks.

- In some programmes the SkillPacks are used in either one or a small number of core units, and in others they are used across all units, with the most appropriate unit for the topic being identified.

- In some programmes there are specific skills units. Skills units initially seem an attractive solution to the problem of coordination across modular courses but students often fail to see the connection between the skills unit and the rest of the course and may not take the skills work seriously. The activities in skills units should be sequenced carefully, so that students can both see their relevance and concentrate on a particular skill at a time when they need to use it elsewhere on the course.

Determining the appropriate level of SkillPack

The levels of the SkillPacks are indicated by a word (Starter and Development) rather than a number to allow flexibility. The development of a skill on some courses may only require the Starter level even towards the end of a course, whereas, on other courses, the Development level might be required at an early stage. The two levels can also allow for differing levels of skill among students at the same stage of a course, and "Identifying Strengths and Improving Skills" was developed partly to help students identify what they needed. In practice the Starter packs have mainly been used at level/year 1 of degree and HND courses in Sheffield Hallam University and the Development packs at levels/years 2 and 3.

Other influential factors

The extensive quantitative and qualitative evaluation of the SkillPack series, carried out with over 2000 staff and students across Sheffield Hallam University, offered some informative cross-tabulations. It was clear that age, gender and educational background could greatly influence response to the Packs and that tutors should be advised to give consideration to the mix of their particular student group. Our findings have implications for how the skills are presented and suggest the need for awareness raising. Some brief examples of the findings are given below.

Educational/employment background

- "Group Work" was more popular with students from further education than those from school.

- "Coping with Pressure" was more popular with those from employment and least popular with those from school.

- "Oral Presentation" was least popular with those from employment.

- As expected, the more traditional study skills were wanted by students who had the least recent experience of academia (eg mature students and those from employment).

Age

- Although it has been said that mature students are less interested in skills development, our evaluation showed otherwise. It was clear that mature students **do** perceive a need here – they are more likely to see the value of the underpinning skills, perhaps because they can place them in context. Consequently, "Managing Yourself and Your Time" and "Negotiating and Assertiveness" were popular with them.

- Students straight from school seemed less likely to recognise the importance of skills which are of more professional rather than academic importance, eg "Report Writing", "Negotiating and Assertiveness".

- "Solving Problems" was least popular with the 18–21 year olds.

Gender

- More women students wanted skills relating to personal, interpersonal and communication skills, eg "Group Work", "Oral Presentation", "Coping with Pressure" and "Managing Yourself and Your Time".

- More men wanted "Revising and Examination Techniques", "Solving Problems" and "Note Taking".

This may indicate differences in values between men and women which may influence how they react to teaching and assessment activities.

1.6 ASSESSMENT

Assessing skills means that:

- students can see they are valued
- the skills become more explicit
- feedback can be provided to help students improve their performance.

1.6.1 Assessment criteria

In order for the above to be realised, students should be made aware of specific assessment criteria relating to skills. Each SkillPack includes the learning outcomes on which it is based (see section 1.9 at the end of this chapter). These can be used as the basis for assessment criteria, perhaps reworded to make them more directly applicable to a specific subject area.

1.6.2 Validity

"Validity" is crucial in assessing skills: the assessment method must be appropriate to the aspect to be assessed. The assessment methods traditionally used in courses may be limited and may be inappropriate for the testing of skills, or they may actually assess something different from the skill targeted. For example: written examinations on skills tend to test an individual's understanding of theories of skill usage rather than their own actual practice of that skill; written reports may be used to assess group projects but they may actually test report writing rather than group working skills.

Methods which are valid for the skills being assessed need to be identified. If students are to be assessed on several skills, the methods used should be varied and consideration should be given to the relationship between the importance of the skill in a given context and the amount of attention given to it in the methods used. For example, assessment methods in a course which rely only on the written word will repeatedly test written rather than verbal or visual communication.

1.6.3 Consistency

"Reliability" in assessment means that a method is capable of producing replicable results. Concerns with accuracy and fairness in assessment has led to an emphasis on this aspect and has tended to limit assessment methods to those which can be accurately replicated, such as those which require one correct answer. Even for topics where there is unlikely to be one correct answer similar types of method have been used, and the concern with reliability has tended to discourage lecturers and tutors from using methods or assessing aspects in which they see "subjectivity" as an issue. This tends to militate against the assessing of skills where there is no one right way to proceed and against assessment methods which, for example, focus on process rather than product.

In reality few subjects have right and wrong answers and, in assessing any sort of work, lecturers and tutors may be influenced by their own values or opinions, or indeed by factors relating to a student, such as the degree of effort put in. In the assessment of skills it seems very important to consider validity as the primary issue and the development of a range of methods which actually test the desired skills. In this context it may be more helpful to think of the issue of reliability in terms of consistency. Are your assessment methods consistent, so that fairness is ensured? Consistency might be encouraged by:

- the use of published assessment criteria

- having clear assessment guides for staff and students

- using consistent procedures; by developing assessment methods which give all students an equal opportunity to demonstrate their skills (eg by avoiding tasks which may discriminate against individuals in respect of gender, age, background or disability).

1.6.4 Feedback

The provision of feedback is very important if students are to use assessment to help them learn how to improve in the future, and if they are to build their confidence. To be most effective in supporting students' skill development, feedback needs to be:

- given as soon after the event as possible (eg soon after a student's oral presentation)

- specific (eg rather it is more helpful to say *"Your visual aids were very clear and used at the right time"* than *"That was a very good presentation"*)

- on something the student can actually do something about (eg not about a physical characteristic or a broad generalisation). Rather than *"You look really unconfident"*, more helpful feedback might be *"You tended to look at your feet and were fidgeting with your hands. You could try using more visual aids to give yourself something to focus on and to give you something to do with your hands. You could scan the audience from time to time"*.

- Having clear assessment criteria helps to make feedback specific. A structured assessment sheet which lists criteria with space for a mark or grade can save time in providing feedback. On such a sheet the preprinted criteria provide the feedback, as they specify the basis on which the mark or grade was given. This can reduce the need for written comments, although they can also be added. Structured feedback sheets improve consistency for one assessor in her/his judgements of students' work and also between assessors where several are involved. **For example:**

✔

Report writing	1	2	3	4	
Clear layout, headings, numbering of sections					*Confused layout, inconsistent headings, no or unclear numbering of sections*
Neat presentation, legible					*Untidy presentation, illegible*
Directed appropriately at the reader and the purpose					*Not clearly directed at the reader or purpose, addresses irrelevant concerns*
Information included is accurate					*Information included is inaccurate*
Standard referencing used, all evidence and information is appropriately referenced					*Inconsistent or incorrect referencing, evidence or information given without sources*
Clear argument, easy to follow, clear recommendations or conclusions					*Argument does not follow clear line, no connections between points, recommendations or conclusions unclear or do not follow on from the previous argument*
Language used is clear, spelling and punctuation follow standard conventions					*Language used is difficult to understand or obscures the meaning, spelling and punctuation do not follow standard conventions*

1.6.5 Self-assessment

Feedback helps students become more aware of how effectively they perform a skill. Asking students to assess their own skill level in some way can also increase their awareness, and this seems to be an important element in encouraging transferability.

Students can, for example, use an assessment sheet, such as the one given above for "Report Writing", and the same sheet can subsequently be used by the tutor to assess the student. This can reveal any discrepancies between what the student thinks is expected and between how s/he judges her/his own performance and what the tutor expects and how the tutor judges the work.

Asking students to evaluate their own performance and to include their evaluation as part of the elements to be assessed can encourage the habit of reflection. The form of such an evaluation could be unstructured and left to the student's discretion, or it could be against criteria either given by the tutor, identified by the students or agreed between the tutor and the students. Students tend to find self-evaluation and assessment difficult and therefore find it helpful to have some guidance, in the form of criteria, for instance.

1.6.6 Peer assessment

The main advantages of peer assessment are:

• students can be a valuable source of additional feedback since other students' feedback comes from a different perspective from that of a tutor

• as a useful method when dealing with large numbers of students – circumstances which make individual feedback from a tutor difficult

• to develop students' critical faculties – providing feedback to others can be a way of helping students identify effective behaviours or performances for themselves

• to provide evaluative information in situations where it is difficult for a lecturer/tutor to do so – for example in group work where a tutor cannot directly observe what is happening.

Care must be taken, however, in introducing and using peer assessment. While students like giving and receiving feedback from peers they may dislike grading or marking other students. When asked to do so (eg by dividing marks between themselves for a group project) they may equalise the marks or mark in a way which benefits themselves. Factors such as peer pressure or a fear of offending their fellow students may be more important to them, for example, than being able to penalise those who do not pull their weight. Peer assessment needs careful handling as it may cause conflict or loss of self esteem (Abson, 1994).

Although students find it helpful to have assessment criteria when assessing their peers, it is also useful for them to think through for themselves what is required, as part of the development of their analytical and critical abilities. One possibility is for a tutor to suggest criteria which can then be discussed by the students and amended or added to.

1.6.7 Assessment methods

For any of the topics covered in this book students could be asked to complete one of the SkillPacks and use it as part of the evidence for the performance of a skill. This might then form part of a portfolio, a collection of material put together for a specific purpose – eg to provide evidence of achievement.

Assessing products

Some of the topics covered by the SkillPacks are easier to assess than others, particularly where there is a clear product. **For example:**

Topic	Assessment criteria can include...	Products to be assessed can include...
Note Taking	*fitness for purpose, clarity, legibility, understandability, identification of main points, accuracy, organisation for ease of retrieval*	*a set of notes taken for a defined purpose, notes taken for a variety of purposes with an evaluation of how they are appropriate for those purposes*
Gathering and Using Information	*use of information which is accurate and relevant to the purpose/audience, accurate recording/citing/referencing of information, identification of key points, accurate use of language/ terminology*	*bibliography, list of references, written/visual/verbal presentations, databases or other computer products, log of sources used, log of reading, book/article reviews, abstracts*
Report Writing Essay Writing	*fitness for the purpose and reader, structure and layout, use of evidence, use of academic conventions such as referencing, effectiveness of argument, use of language or images*	*a report, an essay, a series of drafts with a commentary on revisions, a self-evaluation of the report or essay or a self-completed assessment sheet*
Oral Presentation	*appropriateness for the audience and purpose, evidence of preparation such as speaker's notes, quality of visual aids and expertise in their use, structure of the presentation, delivery, appropriate use of group members for a group presentation, appropriateness of language and manner for the audience, appropriate handling of questions*	*an oral presentation, preparatory materials, visual aids, a self-evaluation of the presentation, evaluation sheets completed by the audience, a video or sound recording of the presentation*
Solving Problems	*thoroughness of research and relevant information gathering, use of problem-solving procedures appropriate for the problem, identification of constraints and other contextual issues, exploration of a range of solutions, appropriateness of the solution for the problem, evaluation of solutions*	*the stages undertaken in a problem-solving process (eg notebooks, drafts, calculations, descriptions, sketches, models/prototypes) with an evaluation of what was effective and what was not, suggestions for how to improve the process in the future, evidence of actual solutions to problems*

Assessment of process

Some skills are more difficult to assess because there is no clear product which indicates the process. In this case methods of assessing can include:

- observing the process

- assessing records or other evidence of the process.

Observation may be difficult, as it may affect the process and may be time-consuming. One example might be group work, where the tutor can either observe a group in action or can participate in a group meeting at a mid-point in a project to review working practices.

The following indicates criteria and some of the evidence which could be gathered to demonstrate the other skill areas covered in this book. Care needs to be taken that the evidence collecting does not become so onerous that it is seen as more significant than the use of the skill itself, as this tends to be demotivating for students and places a heavy workload on staff. Clear indications of boundaries or "quantities" are useful. It is also helpful to encourage reflection in the evidence-collecting process.

Topic	Assessment criteria can include...	Products to be assessed can include...
Organising Yourself and Your Time	*awareness of own practices, use of time management strategies, effectiveness of strategies (eg are deadlines met, is work produced, are agreements realised?)*	*work plans possibly with an evaluation of how effectively they have been followed, meeting deadlines, attendance at meetings (deduction of marks for non-attendance), personal logs/diaries*
Group Work	*agreed group goals, awareness of own behaviour, ability to listen actively and contribute appropriately, doing what has been agreed, attending meetings, participating in meetings, encouraging others*	*minutes of meetings, individual or group evaluations of personal effectiveness or effectiveness as a group (either unstructured or given against criteria), audio tapes of meetings, personal logs/diaries*
Negotiating and Assertiveness	*awareness of own behaviour, use of assertiveness techniques, outcomes of successful negotiations*	*outcomes of negotiation (eg learning contracts, work plans agreed with group members), statements from others, descriptions and evaluations of a particular situation, observed role plays, personal logs/diaries*
Revising and Examination Techniques	*awareness of own behaviour, planning/carrying out revision, covering material appropriately, answering exam questions appropriately and in the time allowed*	*revision timetables, evaluations of what was effective, a review of how the student carried out the exam compared to the tutor's impression of performance*

Confidentiality

As it is most helpful to them if students reflect honestly on their performance, care needs to be taken over confidentiality, particularly where assessment is concerned. Although care needs to be taken with all the topics covered by the SkillPacks two of them – "Coping with Pressure" and "Identifying Strengths and Improving Skills" – are particularly sensitive and need more careful handling if assessed, since they may draw particularly on personal as well as course-based information. Although, clearly, this may be useful and is important for the students, they may be unwilling to reveal to a tutor some of the information asked of them in these SkillPacks. If tutors wish to assess these areas they will need to make the limits of confidentiality very clear – eg that only the tutor will see the information, that the student does not have to provide personal information if he or she prefers not to and that s/he need only provide information s/he feels comfortable with. It may be less personally threatening for the student if the assessment criteria and evidence are linked to a particular situation which is more professional than personal. The following example, taken from a teacher training course, demonstrates this.

Topic	Assessment criteria could include...	Possible evidence could include...
Identifying Strengths and Improving Skills	*self-evaluations of teaching practice, positive response to feedback from colleagues/ student teachers/mentors, support sought from colleagues/student teachers/mentors, areas in need of improvement identified and targets set*	*sections of the worksheet completed with reference to a teaching practice, a self-evaluation, action planning sheet, notes of feedback/advice received, evaluations from colleagues/mentors/pupils, an evaluation of how far the action plan was implemented at a subsequent teaching practice*
Coping with Pressure	*identification of own sources of pressure in teaching and own reactions to them as well as areas to change, support from colleagues/ student teachers/mentors sought and used, positive response to advice, effective handling of pressurising situations, effective handling of combined teaching tasks (eg preparation, classroom practice, assessment, relationships with others)*	*tutor observation of a student's class session with pupils, a personal evaluation identifying sources of and reactions to pressure in teaching, action plans, reviews of progress, an evaluation by teaching practice supervisors*

1.7 SOME EXAMPLES OF USAGE OF THE SKILLPACKS AT SHEFFIELD HALLAM UNIVERSITY

1.7.1 Specific skills units

Example: a Science Programme

This is a first-year skills unit on a programme of over 300 students (HND and degree). The course team identified both those skill areas which they felt confident in delivering and those they felt less sure of and where they would welcome support materials and, for these, four SkillPacks were selected. Students work in groups of six to carry out a group project on a topic of their choice, with supervision from an academic tutor who also acts as personal tutor. Workshops are held at appropriate times to support the skills being used by the students. Assessment of the project is by means of a group oral presentation, a group-produced poster and an individual report by each student. Students are required to submit a portfolio providing evidence of the skills used against the BTEC Common Skills framework (BTEC, 1992).

Example: a Cultural Studies Programme

This is a first-year skills unit on a programme of over 500 students. Students are required to produce a portfolio in which they present evidence of specified skills from the work carried out in other units. This is the mechanism used to integrate the skills unit with the rest of the programme. Thirteen of the SkillPack titles are available to the tutors. The actual content of the sessions varies according to the students' main subject area.

1.7.2 In class time

Example: Combined Studies

First-year exams were due to be taken in six weeks' time. The tutor used the "Revising and Examination Techniques" SkillPack as a basis for discussion. The students worked in groups of three on sections of the Pack and then shared their thoughts and concerns with the whole group.

1.7.3 Integrated into coursework

Example: Mechanical Engineering

First-year students had been working on a project which was to be assessed by an oral presentation. The tutor introduced the SkillPack on "Oral Presentation" during a seminar session and worked through it in relation to the specific task, drawing out those skill elements which were particularly important for the students. The tutor also gave them the criteria for assessment.

Example: Urban Studies

First-year students work in support groups during the Information Management and Presentation unit, in which they are given a task to carry out as a group, along with focused activities for skill development, using the SkillPack titles. Students are required to produce a portfolio of evidence of both their academic work and of their skill development. Both aspects are assessed, and the students are given clear criteria to meet.

Example: Housing Studies

Students carried out a design project in groups of four. The nature of the task was such that its various elements could not be completed by one student in isolation from the other group members. One element was an evaluation of the group process, and students were given the "Group Work" SkillPack and a reading list on group work to help them. A classroom was made available for the groups to meet at a timetabled time, a resource pack was provided and the tutor was available for consultation. The students decided how marks should be allocated between them, although the tutor carried out the assessment. Attendance at group meetings was encouraged by deducting marks from students for unexplained absence.

1.7.4 Combining several SkillPacks

Example: with all seven first-year degree courses in the School of Leisure and Food Management

First-year students were required to work in groups on a research task. Their findings were to be presented as a group report, to be assessed. All the students were given the SkillPacks on "Gathering and Using Information", "Group Work" and "Report Writing" and were required to complete a self-assessment exercise on their skills in both group work and report writing. This carried 15 per cent of their final mark.

1.7.5 Handouts

Example: Education

Before doing a teaching practice, students were given a copy of "Negotiating and Assertiveness" to read in their own time and to refer to when appropriate.

1.7.6 Portfolio assessment

Example: Education

Students must provide evidence that they are able to meet professional standards which are specified by a national body, and are given criteria based on those standards. They complete a portfolio giving evidence of their performance against those criteria, and can include, as part of that evidence, completed copies of relevant SkillPacks.

1.7.7 Sections of the Packs, information adapted

Example: History of Art, Design and Film

In a Research and Presentation Skills unit, the tutor used three SkillPack titles – "Note Taking"; "Gathering and Using Information"; "Report Writing" – and selected sections from each. The complete "Essay Writing" Pack was also given to all students. The selected sections covered those elements of the skill the tutor felt were most relevant to the students. The sections were turned into OHPs and used as a basis for discussion, with the tutor highlighting crucial points and explaining the assessment criteria.

1.7.8 Analysed as text/design

Example: English Studies

Students doing a Skills unit were required to give a five-minute presentation on a SkillPack of their choice. The brief was to explore the use of language in the Pack, the content, presentation and relevance. This exercise was not part of the final assessment.

1.7.9 Reference in the University libraries

A full set of SkillPacks is held on reference in all five of Sheffield Hallam University libraries, and in the Careers and Counselling Service information room.

1.7.10 For individual students

Individual students who are experiencing difficulties with a particular skill have been given the appropriate Pack(s) by their tutor – eg "Organising Yourself and Your Time", "Coping with Pressure", "Revising and Examination Techniques". The tutor has drawn the student's attention to those aspects of the skill which he or she needs to work on, and has then asked the student to draw up an Action Plan for the tutor to see.

1.7.11 Drop-in skills course

Example: Management Sciences course for Applied Statistics and Systems Modelling

Because the first-year tutors felt that their students needed more in the way of skill development, a two-day non-compulsory course was held during the transition week between the first and second semesters. Students signed up for whichever session interested them and tutors used the appropriate SkillPacks as a basis for discussion and activity, supplementing them with other material – eg videos and tapes. All the Packs were available to students as handouts to study in their own time.

1.8 SUMMARY

This book supports teaching staff, by providing materials which they can use to help students develop a range of skills. Students' improved performance in these areas will not only help them be more successful on their courses, but will lay the foundations for skills which are needed at work. This should also make the task of lecturers and tutors easier – eg by improving the presentation of work submitted and therefore aiding the assessment process, or by improving students' time management so that work is handed in when expected.

The materials support students in continually improving and developing their performance – their "lifelong learning". They aim not only to provide numerous practical suggestions but also to encourage the practice of reflection and enhance self-awareness.

1.9 LEARNING OUTCOMES

The following gives the learning outcomes on which the SkillPacks are based. These should be helpful to academic staff in:

• providing a starting point for the production of assessment criteria

• clarifying to students what is required

• helping to identify the appropriate level of skill.

The identification of the outcomes greatly facilitated the writing of the SkillPacks.

The learning outcomes are based on the NCVQ Core Skills specification at their level 3 (our Starter level) and 4 (our Development level), but are related to more specific tasks than are the NCVQ specifications (eg report writing, rather than written communication). Differentiation of level between the Starter and Development SkillPacks is based on:

• a widening repertoire of aspects of the skill

• use of the skill in widening contexts

• increasing autonomy in the use of the skills.

"Note Taking" is at Starter level only, as the Development level outcomes proved to be similar to those for "Gathering and Using Information".

The learning outcomes cover the following titles:

• "Identifying Strengths and Improving Skills"

• "Organising Yourself and Your Time"

• "Note Taking"

• "Gathering and Using Information"

• "Essay Writing"

• "Report Writing"

• "Oral Presentation"

• "Solving Problems"

• "Group Work"

• "Negotiating and Assertiveness"

• "Coping with Pressure"

• "Revising and Examination Techniques".

1.9.1 Identifying Strengths and Improving Skills: Learning Outcomes Specification

The levels are differentiated by:

- **a widening repertoire of skills**
- **a widening context**
- **greater autonomy in deciding how to use the skills.**

The learning outcomes can be related to the NCVQ Core Skill specifications at their levels 3 (Starter Pack) and 4 (Development Pack). This should not be seen as limiting. Students working on Starter Pack outcomes may be working towards Development Pack outcomes.

Starter Pack: learning outcomes	Development Pack: learning outcomes
Students are able to:	Students are able to:
1 identify their own strengths and weaknesses, based on appropriate evidence	1 identify their own strengths and weaknesses, based on appropriate evidence
2 identify development needs and set targets for improving skill areas	2 identify development needs, set targets for improving skill areas, and review and revise those targets according to changing circumstances
3 use feedback constructively	3 actively seek and use feedback constructively and regularly
4 seek and use appropriate support	4 select activities to improve skill performance which are appropriate to own strengths and weaknesses and to the circumstances
	5 acknowledge own responsibility for skill development, whilst seeking and using appropriate support
Range	**Range**
Context: the units studied	Context: the units studied and the professional area
Level of support and feedback: periods of intensive support and feedback with periods of reduced support and feedback	Levels of support and feedback: periods of intense and reduced support and feedback, periods of self-directed learning
Points where support and feedback are required: determined by others and self	Points where support and feedback are required: determined by others and self
Sources of feedback: lecturers, peers, learning materials (eg video, written)	Sources of feedback: lecturers, peers, employers or outside contacts, learning materials (eg video, written)

1.9.2 Organising Yourself and Your Time: Learning Outcomes Specification

The levels are differentiated by:

- **a widening repertoire of skills**
- **a widening context**
- **greater autonomy in deciding how to use the skills.**

The learning outcomes can be related to the NCVQ Core Skill specifications at their levels 3 (Starter Pack) and 4 (Development Pack). This should not be seen as limiting. Students working on Starter Pack outcomes may be working towards Development Pack outcomes.

Starter Pack: learning outcomes	Development Pack: learning outcomes
Students are able to:	Students are able to:
1 identify own current practices in organising self and time, and the strengths and weaknesses of those practices	1 identify own current practices in organising self and time, and the strengths and weaknesses of those practices
2 identify aims and targets	2 identify aims and targets
3 identify and explore strategies and resources for organising self and time	3 identify and explore strategies and resources (eg delegation) for organising self and time in order to maximise effectiveness
4 select and use strategies to meet aims, targets, deadlines	4 select and use strategies to maximise opportunities to meet aims, targets, deadlines
5 identify and use feedback and support	5 identify and use feedback
6 respond effectively to current pressures	6 respond effectively to current pressures and plan ahead to meet future pressures
Range	**Range**
Context: the course/programme units	Context: the course/programme units or professional area
Complexity of situation: anticipated, limited number of demands	Complexity of situation: unanticipated, several conflicting demands
Level of support: periods of intensive support	Level of support: periods of reduced support; periods of self-direction

1.9.3 Note Taking: Learning Outcomes Specification

The Starter Pack learning outcomes can be related to the NCVQ Core Skill specifications at their level 3.

Starter Pack: learning outcomes
Students are able to: 1 identify the purpose to which the notes will be put 2 identify main points 3 accurately identify the meaning of unfamiliar words, phrases and images 4 record images which provide a clear illustration of the points 5 accurately record sources of information 6 produce notes which are legible, well structured, and well organised for retrieval 7 use notes for the purpose for which they were intended
Range Context/audience: self; peers Subject: covered by the course; notes from oral, visual, printed, or computerised sources Format: written, images, IT

1.9.4 Gathering and Using Information: Learning Outcomes Specification

The levels are differentiated by:

- **a widening repertoire of skills**
- **a widening context**
- **greater autonomy in deciding how to use the skills.**

The learning outcomes can be related to the NCVQ Core Skill specifications at their levels 3 (Starter Pack) and 4 (Development Pack). This should not be seen as limiting. Students working on Starter Pack outcomes may be working towards Development Pack outcomes.

Starter Pack: learning outcomes	Development Pack: learning outcomes
Students are able to:	Students are able to:
1 find sources of information relevant to and sufficient for the purpose and audience	1 find sources of information relevant to and sufficient for the purpose and audience
2 use effective reading and observing strategies eg skimming, scanning, in-depth reading or viewing	2 use effective reading and observing strategies eg skimming, scanning, in-depth reading or viewing
3 identify the meaning of subject specific terminology as used in the programme units studied	3 identify the meaning of subject specific terminology as used in the programme units studied and in the professional area
4 identify the main points or issues of relevance to the topic	4 identify the main points or issues of relevance to the topic
5 accurately record sources of information	5 accurately record sources of information
	6 identify factors which influence the interpretation of the information, identifying any reasons for bias or distortion
	7 criticise and evaluate the information, using supporting evidence
Range	**Range**
Subject matter, purposes, audience: relevant to the programme units taken	Subject matter, purpose, audience: relevant to the programme units studied and the professional area
Format: written material (books, articles, reports, publicity materials, brochures), visual material (graphs, video, film, photography, works of art/design), computerised material	Format: written material (books, articles, reports, publicity materials, brochures), visual material (graphs, video, film, photography, works of art/design), computerised material
Sources of clarification: libraries, reference books, tutors, peers	Sources of clarification: libraries, reference books, tutors, peers, outside organisations or individuals

1.9.5 Essay Writing: Learning Outcomes Specification

The levels are differentiated by:

* **a widening repertoire of skills**
* **a widening context**
* **greater autonomy in deciding how to use the skills.**

The learning outcomes can be related to the NCVQ Core Skill specifications at their levels 3 (Starter Pack) and 4 (Development Pack). This should not be seen as limiting. Students working on Starter Pack outcomes may be working towards Development Pack outcomes.

Starter Pack: learning outcomes	Development Pack: learning outcomes
Students are able to:	Students are able to:
1 present the essay in a clearly structured form, appropriate for purpose and audience	1 present the essay in a clearly structured form, appropriate for purpose and audience
2 produce a sequenced argument, reflected in the logical structure of the essay	2 produce a sequenced argument, reflected in the logical structure of the essay
3 plan strategies for producing the essay	3 plan strategies for producing the essay and criticise those plans
4 act on understanding of the explicit and implicit tasks within the title	4 act on understanding of the explicit and implicit tasks within the title and critically review the essay question
5 gather, sort and present evidence to substantiate a case, using appropriate referencing techniques	5 gather, sort and present evidence to substantiate a case, using appropriate referencing techniques
6 follow standard conventions for grammar, spelling and punctuation	6 follow standard conventions for grammar, spelling and punctuation
7 use appropriate conventions of academic presentation	7 use appropriate conventions of academic presentation
8 comply with the University's regulations on plagiarism	8 comply with the University's regulations on plagiarism
9 proofread, edit and review the work	9 critically evaluate the effectiveness of the final product and identify areas for future improvement
10 use feedback to improve performance	10 use feedback to improve performance
Range	**Range**
Subject, purpose: relevant to the programme studied	Subject, purpose: relevant to the programme studied
Audience: tutor, students	Audience: tutor, students
Level of support: periods of specific guidance	Levels of support: periods of reduced guidance, periods of self-direction

1.9.6 Report Writing: Learning Outcomes Specification

The levels are differentiated by:

- **a widening repertoire of skills**
- **a widening context**
- **greater autonomy in deciding how to use the skills.**

The learning outcomes can be related to the NCVQ Core Skill specifications at their levels 3 (Starter Pack) and 4 (Development Pack). This should not be seen as limiting. Students working on Starter Pack outcomes may be working towards Development Pack outcomes.

Starter Pack: learning outcomes	Development Pack: learning outcomes
Students are able to:	Students are able to:
1 identify the purpose of the report and the needs and characteristics of the audience	1 identify the purpose of the report and the needs and characteristics of the audience
2 include accurate information appropriate to the purpose and audience	2 include accurate information appropriate to the purpose and audience, and criticise and evaluate the information, identifying reasons for any bias or distortion
3 produce a report in a format appropriate to the subject area, purpose and audience, and present it legibly, with a clear layout	3 decide on and use a format appropriate to the subject area, purpose and audience, present it legibly and with a clear layout
4 use images to support or clarify main points	4 use images to support or clarify main points
5 use language which is appropriate for the subject area, purpose and audience and use grammar, punctuation and spelling which follow standard conventions	5 use language which is appropriate for the subject area, purpose and audience and use grammar, punctuation and spelling which follow standard conventions
	6 clearly signpost for the audience the critical points or issues
	7 evaluate the effectiveness of the report for the purpose and audience and identify areas for future improvement
Range	**Range**
Subject, purpose: relevant to the programme units studied	Subject, purpose: relevant to the programme units studied and the professional area
Audience: students, tutor, familiar/unfamiliar with the subject matter	Audience: students, tutor, familiar/unfamiliar with the subject matter, members of professional or outside organisations, members of the public
Format: predetermined format	Format: appropriate for subject, purpose and audience

1.9.7 Oral Presentation: Learning Outcomes Specification

The levels are differentiated by:

- **a widening repertoire of skills**
- **a widening context**
- **greater autonomy in deciding how to use the skills.**

The learning outcomes can be related to the NCVQ Core Skill specifications at their levels 3 (Starter Pack) and 4 (Development Pack). This should not be seen as limiting. Students working on Starter Pack outcomes may be working towards Development Pack outcomes.

Starter Pack: learning outcomes	Development Pack: learning outcomes
Students are able to:	Students are able to:
1 select material which is appropriate for the purpose and the audience	1 select material which is appropriate for the purpose and the audience
2 structure material for the purpose and the audience	2 structure material for the purpose and the audience
3 prepare relevant visual aids which clearly illustrate points (eg legible OHP slides)	3 prepare relevant visual aids which clearly illustrate points (eg legible OHP slides)
4 present visual aids effectively and at appropriate junctures	4 present visual aids effectively and at appropriate junctures
5 use language, tone and manner (including non-verbal behaviour) suited to the purpose and audience	5 use language, tone and manner (including non verbal behaviour) suited to the purpose and audience, and which draw on the presenter's personal style
6 listen to and effectively answer questions	6 encourage audience participation (eg questions) and respond effectively
7 for group presentations, allocate tasks so each member has a role	7 actively check audience understanding, observe audience reaction and make appropriate responses
	8 for group presentations, allocate tasks which make best use of individual abilities and expertise
Range	**Range**
Subject matter, purpose: relevant to the programme units studied	Subject matter, purpose: relevant to the units studied and the professional area
Audience: tutors, other students; familiar/unfamiliar with the topic	Audience: tutors, other students, familiar/unfamiliar with the topic, members of outside organisations or of the public
Format: seminar presentations, individual or group presentations of project work, critiques or oral assessment	Format: seminar presentations, individual or group presentations of project work, critiques or oral assessment
Sources of clarification: tutors, other students, videos/materials on oral presentation skills	Sources of clarification: tutors, students, videos/materials on oral presentation skills, the audience

1.9.8 Solving Problems: Learning Outcomes Specification

The levels are differentiated by:

- **a widening repertoire of skills**
- **a widening context**
- **greater autonomy in deciding how to use the skills.**

The learning outcomes can be related to the NCVQ Core Skill specifications at their levels 3 (Starter Pack) and 4 (Development Pack). The levels should not be seen as limiting. Students working on Starter Pack outcomes may be working towards Development Pack outcomes.

Starter Pack: learning outcomes	Development Pack: learning outcomes
Students are able to:	Students are able to:
1 collect sufficient information to • clarify critical features of the problem • identify possible solutions	1 collect information and regularly review it to identify where more is needed to • clarify critical features • identify possible solutions
2 select relevant information	2 select relevant information, investigate contradictory information and identify reasons for it
3 identify critical features of problems which include a broad range of factors and a range of possible solutions	3 identify critical features of problems which include a broad range of factors and a range of possible solutions and where there is a significant amount of contradictory information
4 where appropriate, accurately follow set procedures to clarify the problem, seek information and identify solutions	4 where appropriate, accurately follow set procedures to clarify the problem, seek information and identify solutions
5 identify and select efficient and effective procedures to clarify the problem, seek information and identify solutions	5 identify and select efficient and effective procedures to clarify the problem, seek information and identify solutions. Identify general rules to help clarify the problem or select solutions
6 identify and use criteria to select an effective solution (eg short-term and long-term benefits)	6 identify and use criteria to select an effective solution (eg short-term and long-term benefits)
Range Context/subject: within the programme units	**Range** Context/subject: within the programme units and the professional area
Complexity of problem: limited factors with one preferred solution achievable by following set procedures; broad range of factors and a range of possible solutions	Complexity of problem: limited factors with one preferred solution achievable by following set procedures; broad range of factors and a range of possible solutions; including a substantial amount of contradictory information
Procedures: critical features of the problem are already identified as are set procedures; individuals must identify and select procedures themselves with guidance	Procedures: critical features of the problem are already identified as are set procedures; individuals must identify and select procedures themselves

1.9.9 Group Work: Learning Outcomes Specification

The levels are differentiated by:

- **a widening repertoire of skills**
- **a widening context**
- **greater autonomy in deciding how to use the skills.**

The learning outcomes can be related to the NCVQ Core Skill specifications at their levels 3 (Starter Pack) and 4 (Development Pack). This should not be seen as limiting. Students working on Starter Pack outcomes may be working towards Development Pack outcomes.

Starter Pack: learning outcomes	Development Pack: learning outcomes
Students are able to:	Students are able to:
1 clarify and understand group goals	1 clarify, agree and understand group goals. Consider and agree relevant basic principles
2 plan actions to meet goals and review group and individual progress	2 plan action to meet goals, and review group and individual progress. Review and agree amendments to goals and plans as necessary
3 agree allocation of tasks	3 agree allocation of tasks, taking into account individual skills and knowledge and encouraging flexibility. Agree appropriate leadership if needed
4 carry them out within agreed limits	4 carry out tasks within agreed limits, using the different perspectives of other group members to improve personal performance
5 contribute to meetings in a way which is relevant and equal	5 contribute to meetings in a way which is relevant, equal and draws on personal skills and knowledge
6 listen actively to others	6 actively seek and listen to the contributions of others
7 request feedback on individual performance (relating to tasks and behaviour)	7 request feedback on individual performance (relating to task and behaviour)
8 identify elements of personal behaviour which are effective or less effective in a group situation	8 identify elements of personal performance which are effective or less effective in a range of group situations. Plan action to implement appropriate behaviour
Range	**Range**
Subject matter: related to the programme units studied	Subject matter: related to the programme units studied and the professional area
Purpose: goals are given by the tutor or agreed by the group and the tutor	Purpose: goals are determined for the group or by the group itself
Feedback and sources of support: group members, tutor	Feedback and sources of support: group members, tutor, members of outside organisations

1.9.10 Negotiating and Assertiveness: Learning Outcomes Specification

The levels are differentiated by:

- **a widening repertoire of skills**
- **a widening context**
- **greater autonomy in deciding how to use the skills.**

The learning outcomes can be related to the NCVQ Core Skill specifications at their levels 3 (Starter Pack) and 4 (Development Pack). This should not be seen as limiting. Students working on Starter Pack outcomes may be working towards Development Pack outcomes.

Starter Pack: learning outcomes	Development Pack: learning outcomes
Students are able to:	Students are able to:
1 identify own needs, goals, responsibilities and rights	1 identify own needs, goals, responsibilities and rights; check on others' understanding of own position
2 clarify own understanding of others' needs, goals, responsibilities and rights	2 clarify own understanding of others' needs, goals, responsibilities and rights
3 know of strategies to use and their possible effects	3 know of strategies to use and their possible effects and anticipate their possible effects in a given situation
4 implement strategies in given situations and review their effectiveness in terms of meeting goals which are mutually acceptable	4 implement strategies in given situations and review their effectiveness in terms of meeting goals which are mutually acceptable
	5 identify strengths and weaknesses of own negotiating with others, and identify actions to build on strengths and improve weaknesses
	6 monitor progress on actions identified and review goals
Range	**Range**
Context: with peers on the programme units; anticipated/routine situations	Context/audience: with peers and tutors on the programme units and with members of outside organisations; unexpected non-routine situations
Mode: face-to-face, telephone	Mode: face-to-face, telephone

1.9.11 Coping with Pressure: Learning Outcomes Specification

The levels are differentiated by:

- **a widening repertoire of skills**
- **a widening context**
- **greater autonomy in deciding how to use the skills.**

The learning outcomes can be related to the NCVQ Core Skill specifications at their levels 3 (Starter Pack) and 4 (Development Pack). This should not be seen as limiting. Students working on Starter Pack outcomes may be working towards Development Pack outcomes.

Starter Pack: learning outcomes	Development Pack: learning outcomes
Students are able to:	Students are able to:
1 identify, seeking feedback from others, own reactions and usual responses to pressure	1 identify, seeking feedback from others, own reactions and usual responses to pressure, and recognise signals of own stress at an early stage
2 identify sources of pressure	2 anticipate and identify possible sources of pressure at an early stage
3 evaluate the effectiveness of own reactions and responses, and identify needs for change	3 monitor the effectiveness of own reactions and responses, and identify needs for change
4 plan short-term goals related to needs for change, and plan actions needed	4 plan short-term goals and actions to allow for changing circumstances
5 identify and use sources of support	5 identify at what point there is need for support and actively seek and use it
6 put plans into action, record and review progress	6 put plans into action, record and review progress in relation to changing circumstances
Range Context: the programme units studied Feedback and support: students, tutors, university support agencies, learning materials	**Range** Context: the whole student experience Feedback and support: students, tutors, university support agencies, learning materials, outside support agencies

1.9.12 Revising and Examination Techniques: Learning Outcomes Specification

The levels are differentiated by:

- **a widening repertoire of skills**
- **a widening context**
- **greater autonomy in deciding how to use the skills.**

The learning outcomes can be related to the NCVQ Core Skill specifications at their levels 3 (Starter Pack) and 4 (Development Pack). The levels should not be seen as limiting. Students working on Starter Pack outcomes may be working towards Development Pack outcomes.

Starter Pack: learning outcomes	Development Pack: learning outcomes
Students are able to:	Students are able to:
1 identify the purpose and format of the examination and what the examiners are seeking	1 identify the purpose and format of the examination, what the examiners are seeking (including external examiners)
2 identify which material to revise	2 identify and prioritise which material to revise
3 identify from a range of revision techniques which ones are best suited to self, the material and the format of the exam	3 identify which of the revision techniques used to date are best suited to self, the material and the format of the exam
4 plan actions and the time required for revision, within given constraints	4 plan actions and the time required for revision within given constraints and allowing for own strengths and weaknesses
5 monitor progress and amend plans	5 monitor progress and review original goals and amend plans
6 identify own usual reactions and responses to the examination situation, and plan for them	6 identify own usual reactions and responses to the examination situation and plan strategies to improve performance
7 identify what the question means and analyse what is required	7 identify what the question means and analyse what is required
8 identify which questions to answer in which order, and plan time allocation	8 identify which questions to answer in an order which will maximise performance
9 plan answers which include appropriate evidence	9 plan answers which include appropriate evidence, evaluation and criticism of that evidence
10 review own revision and examination strategies and identify improved methods for the future	10 review own revision and examination strategies and identify improved methods for the future
Range	**Range**
Subject, purpose: related to the programme units studied	Subject, purpose: related to the programme units studied
Context: early stages of a programme	Context: final stages of a programme
Audience: tutors	Audience: tutors, external examiners

1.10 REFERENCES

Abson, D. (1994), "The effects of peer evaluation on the behaviour of undergraduate students working in tutorless groups" in Foot, H.C. Howe, C.J. Anderson, A. Tolmie, A.K. and Warden, D.A. (eds), *Group and Interactive Learning*. Computational Mechanic's Publications.

Association of Graduate Recruiters (1993), *Roles for Graduates in the 21st Century. Getting the Balance Right*, AGR.

Becker, H.S. Beer, B. and Hughes, E. (1968), *Making the Grade. The Academic Side of College*, John Wiley.

Business and Technical Education Council (1992), *Common Skills and Core Themes. General Guidelines*, BTEC.

Confederation of British Industry (1989), *Towards a Skills Revolution*, CBI.

Council for National Academic Awards (1989), *CNAA Handbook*, CNAA.

Department of Education and Science (1985), *Better Schools*, Cmnd 9469, HMSO

Department of Education and Science (1985), *The Development of Higher Education into the 1990s*, Cmnd 9524, HMSO.

Department of Education and Science (1986), *Working Together – Education and Training*, Cmnd 9823, HMSO.

Department of Education and Science (1987), *Higher Education – Meeting the Challenge*, Cmnd 114, HMSO.

Kolb, D.A. (1984), *Experiential Learning*, Prentice Hall.

Manpower Services Commission (1981), *A New Training Initiative. A Consultative Document*, MSC.

Marton, F. and Saljo, R. (1984), "Approaches to learning" in Marton, F. Hounsell, D. and Entwistle, N. *The Experience of Learning*, Scottish Academic Press.

National Advisory Body (1986), *Transferable Skills in Employment – The Contribution of Higher Education*, NAB.

National Curriculum Council (1990), *Core Skills 16–19*, NCC.

Oates, T. (1992a), "Core Skills and transfer: aiming high", *Educational and Training Technology International*, **29** (3), pp.227–39.

Oates, T. (1992b), *Developing and Piloting the NCVQ Core Skill Units. An Outline of Method and a Summary of Findings*, NCVQ.

Schon, D.A. (1987), *Educating the Reflective Practitioner*, Jossey Bass.

Trades Union Congress (1989), *Skills 2000*, TUC.

PART I

STARTER LEVEL SKILLPACKS

2
IDENTIFYING STRENGTHS AND IMPROVING SKILLS

by Sue Drew and Rosie Bingham

CONTENTS

"I just want to get on with the course. Why bother thinking about myself?"

Taking stock, identifying what you are good at and what you need to improve should make you feel more confident about your strengths, help you work out how to do things better, and improve your performance on the course.

"Leopards can't change their spots. Old dogs can't learn new tricks."

This SkillPack is based on a different view – that people **can** and **do** change.

We suggest you use this SkillPack:

- to diagnose your current skill level
- to identify evidence of your abilities (important if you are asked to demonstrate that you have a skill for coursework assessment, or if you are applying for placements or jobs)
- to identify which other SkillPacks in this series might help you and which actions to take to improve your skills.

When you have completed it, you will be able to:

1 identify your own strengths and weaknesses, based on appropriate evidence
2 identify development needs and set targets for improving skill areas
3 use feedback constructively
4 seek and use appropriate support.

You should be able to use this skill in your course/programme, with support from others, and using feedback from lecturers/tutors, and other students.

2.1 YOUR CURRENT SKILLS

2.1.1 Guide to completing the following Skill Diagnosis Sheet

In identifying your skills, it helps to think of a particular situation. *"What am I good at?"* is more difficult to answer than *"What did working on that project/laboratory experiment/essay show that I was good at?"*

We suggest that you list your recent course activities (eg projects, seminars, tutorials, oral presentations, research, producing essays or reports etc) in the box below.

Course activities

We then suggest you complete the Skill Diagnosis Sheet in Section 2.1.3 whilst thinking about those course activities. It is based on all the other available SkillPacks.

For example:

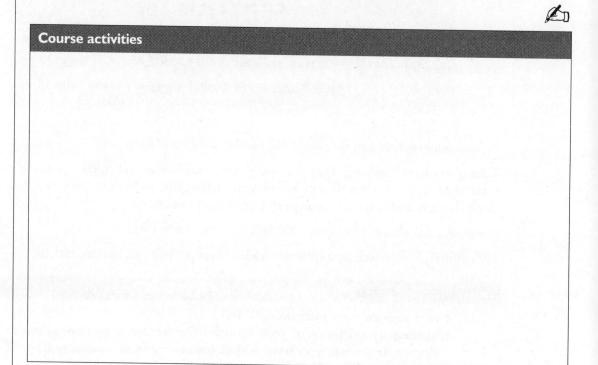

Current level					
Skill area	1	2	3	4	**Evidence and examples**
	High			**Low**	
Organising yourself and your time				✔	*Failed to meet deadlines, had to stay up all night to get work done.*
Negotiating and assertiveness		✔			*Group project, managed to get others to pull their weight most (but not all) of the time.*
Oral presentation	✔				*Gave presentation to course group. Received good feedback, especially on visual aids. Got high grade. Felt confident.*

2.1.2 Seeking feedback

In completing the Skill Diagnosis Sheet you may find it helpful to ask others (eg tutors, friends, fellow students) for feedback about your skills. It helps to ask specific questions.

- *"How do you think I coped with the pressure of the exams?"* could elicit useful information (eg *"You seemed to leave things until the last minute and then got quite tense about it"*).

- *"Can I cope with stress?"* This is a more general question which may lead to sweeping statements in reply. It invites judgemental comments which may be less helpful *(eg "Yes, very well"; "No, you go to pieces")*.

When seeking feedback it helps to:

- **listen without interrupting or defending**
- **check that you have understood** (*"Do you mean that …?"*)
- **weigh up which aspects of the feedback you agree with and what to take note of (you may think the other person is wrong or has misunderstood the situation).**

2.1.3 The Skill Diagnosis Sheet

On the following Skill Diagnosis Sheets please estimate:

- **your current level of skill on a four-point scale where 1 = very good and 4 = in need of considerable improvement**
- **your need for improvement on a four-point scale, where 1 = very important to improve and 4 = not important to improve.**

(For example, if your skill level is low in a certain area, you could consider it very important for you to improve it, or you could think that, on your particular course, it does not really matter).

Although the Skill Diagnosis Sheet is based on all the other SkillPacks available – feel free to add other skills to the list which are important to you or your course.

NOTES

Skill	Your estimate of your current level of skill				Evidence and examples (why you have rated your current skill level as you have)	Priority for improvement			
	1 high	2	3	4 low		1 high	2	3	4 low
Organising yourself and your time									
Note taking									
Gathering and using information									
Essay writing									

Skill	Your estimate of your current level of skill				Evidence and examples (why you have rated your current skill level as you have)	Priority for improvement			
	1 high	2	3	4 low		1 high	2	3	4 low
Report writing									
Oral presentation									
Solving problems									
Group work									

NOTES

NOTES

Skill	Your estimate of your current level of skill				Evidence and examples (why you have rated your current skill level as you have)	Priority for improvement			
	1 high	2	3	4 low		1 high	2	3	4 low
Negotiating and assertiveness									
Coping with pressure									
Revising and examination techniques									
Others (please specify)									

2.2 DEVELOPING YOUR SKILLS: ACTION PLANNING AND SEEKING HELP

2.2.1 Guide to completing the following Action Planning Sheet

How could you develop your skills? Being as specific as possible about where you need to improve is a first step.

- **Sometimes this makes the solution obvious** – eg if you felt stressed because you started exam revision too late, you can plan to begin earlier in future.
- **Sometimes you may need to seek advice.** Using the example of exam revision, you may need advice from a tutor about prioritising what to revise.
- **Sometimes you may need more help** – eg some people feel so nervous about exams that they may need to talk it over with a specialist who can help.

We suggest that you complete the Action Planning Sheet in Section 2.2.3 and (very important) that you review it with somebody else (eg with a friend) in, say, a month's time to see what action you have actually taken.

For example:

Skill	What I can do	Where I could seek help	I will do this by
Problem solving	*Think about the problem before launching into it. Try to identify the main issues first.*	*The "Solving Problems" SkillPack.* *If others also find it difficult, ask a lecturer to cover it.* *Ask other students how they deal with similar problems.* *Look at relevant material in your university or college library.*	*next week (we suggest you give a date)* *next week* *in 2 weeks* *in 3 weeks*

2.2.2 Possible sources of help

- **Other SkillPacks.** There are SkillPacks on all the areas listed on the Skill Diagnosis Sheets.

- **Libraries.** Check if your university or college library has material under the general "study skills" title.

- **Your lecturers.** They may be able to spend some time in class on a particular skill area.

- **Friends and other students** – either from your year, or in later years (where they have experienced the stage you are at). What ideas do they have for improving the skill?

In addition, your university or college may be able to offer you:

- **study skills courses**
- **counselling services**
- **careers services.**

NOTES

NOTES

2.2.3 Action Planning Sheet

Skills I wish to focus on	What I can do	Where I could seek help	By (a target deadline helps)

2.3 REFERENCES AND BIBLIOGRAPHY

University and college libraries and careers services may have materials on this skill. The following give examples:

AGCAS (1992), *Where Next? Exploring your Future,* (a series of booklets) AGCAS.

Booklet 1   "Taking the plunge"
Booklet 2   "Reflections"
Booklet 3   "Sharpening the image"
Booklet 4   "Choices"

AGCAS (1992) *Discovering Yourself. A Self-assessment Guide for Older Students,* AGCAS.

3
ORGANISING YOURSELF AND YOUR TIME

by Sue Drew and Rosie Bingham

CONTENTS

This SkillPack aims to help you organise yourself to ensure you can meet the course requirements and to give yourself a good chance of performing well.

As a student in university or college you are expected to do a lot of work outside class activities and the responsibility to succeed is placed in your hands. In other words, you are given assignments but it is up to you when and how you carry them out. You will also be expected to read around your subject but how much you do will be up to you.

This may be very different from school where teachers may exert pressure on you to work, or from employment, where managers may determine your workload.

Students need to balance different activities: social life; domestic commitments; work; the course. The evidence suggests that organised students do better than disorganised ones, and that students think this is a very important skill to develop.

We suggest you use this SkillPack:

- **to help you plan your work over the next few weeks or over the coming semester.**

When you have completed it, you will be able to:

1 identify your own current practices in organising yourself and your time, and the strengths and weaknesses of those practices
2 identify aims and targets
3 identify and explore strategies and resources for organising yourself and your time
4 select and use strategies to meet aims, targets and deadlines
5 identify and use feedback and support
6 respond effectively to current pressures.

You should be able to use this skill on your course/programme in cases where you can anticipate the situations in which you need to organise yourself and your time and in which you have a limited number of demands, and with support from lecturers/tutors and others.

3.1 HOW YOU CURRENTLY SPEND YOUR TIME

Keeping a diary of your activities for a week helps you appreciate how you spend your time. You could use the following chart either:

• **to record your activities as you go,** or
• **retrospectively at the end of each day or at the end of the week.**

We suggest you select a four- or five- hour period in one day to record activities in more detail in 15-minute blocks.

Time	Mon	Tues	Wed	Thurs	Fri	Sat	Sun
7-8 am							
8-9 am							
9-10 am							
10-11 am							
11-12 am							
12-1 pm							
1-2 pm							
2-3 pm							
3-4 pm							
4-5 pm							

NOTES

Time	Mon	Tues	Wed	Thurs	Fri	Sat	Sun
5-6 pm							
6-7 pm							
7-8 pm							
8-9 pm							
9-10 pm							
10-11 pm							
11-12 pm							
12-1 am							
1-2 am							
2-3 am							
3-4 am							
4-5 am							
5-6 am							
6-7 am							

You can now consider:

NOTES

Why did I spend my time in that way?

Is the way I spend my time helping me to study efficiently? What is good about how I use time?

Am I surprised by anything?

Do I need to change anything? What?

Is there anything I really can't change? What?

You might find it useful to discuss your diary and responses to these questions with others. Their feedback may be very helpful.

NOTES

3.2 HOW YOU CURRENTLY ORGANISE YOUR WORK

	Yes	No
Are your notes: • in piles on the floor? • on the floor, not in piles? • filed systematically?		
Could you quickly find notes for a piece of work you did two months ago?		
Can you find equipment quickly (eg pens, calculator, files, paperclips)?		
Have you got a workspace/desk?		
Is there any space on your workspace/desk or it is cluttered?		
Do you have a reminder system for what you need to do?		

Giving attention to your organisation can save you hours of wasted time. It is well worth spending half a day setting up systems which suit you (it's no good having elaborate systems you won't stick to) and a couple of hours a week to maintain it or have a "sort out".

How could you improve your organisation, given any constraints related to where you live (at home, shared accommodation etc)? You could get feedback from friends about their views on how well (or not) you are organised. How do they do things?

NOTES

3.3 IDENTIFYING TARGETS

An important first step is to identify what you have to do by when. It is helpful to start by looking at an overall target and then breaking it down into smaller tasks. How long will each sub-task take? Have you allowed for potential problems, such as everybody else wanting the same book or everybody else wanting access to computers? You should give actual dates in the deadline column below.

For example:

Main target	Deadline	Estimated time to complete
Write an essay	*Two months away*	*6 weeks*

Sub-tasks	Deadline	Estimated time to complete
Gather information	*1 month away*	*3 weeks*
Write first draft	*6 weeks away*	*1 week*
Final editing and final draft	*2 months away*	*3 days*

Main target	Deadline	Estimated time to complete

Sub-tasks	Deadline	Estimated time to complete

3.4 STRATEGIES FOR ORGANISING YOURSELF AND YOUR TIME

3.4.1 Prioritising

It is likely that you will have several pieces of work to do together, all with similar deadlines. You may also have non-course commitments or interests to fit in. How will you ensure that it all gets done? The following suggestions cover a range of strategies:

• **Plan it out on a big piece of paper and tick off items as they are completed.**

• **Prioritise using the following system:**

1 urgent and important – do it now
2 urgent but not important – do it if you can
3 important but not urgent – start it before it becomes urgent
4 not important and not urgent – don't do it.

• **Have three trays and a waste bin.** Allocate one tray for each of 1, 2, 3 above and throw category 4 into the bin.

• **Make out a list with the most important things first.**

• **Identify which are your strongest and which are your weakest subjects.** Should you allocate equal time to each, or more to the weaker one? Possible dangers are:

– avoiding giving time to topics you dislike or feel weak at
– spending so much time on them you neglect areas you are good at.

Is the time you are spending on something equal to its importance?

• **Build in breaks** – a coffee, a walk around the block, watching the news.

• **Reward yourself with a treat when you have achieved a target (or part of a target).**

• **Allow for unforeseen circumstances (a full bus, a long queue at the library etc) and build in leeway.**

• **Make quick decisions about what action to take.** Repeatedly picking up the same piece of paper wastes time.

3.4.2 Time wasters

The following is a list of possible time wasters. You may wish to eliminate some altogether. Others may be enjoyable but detract from time available for study and you may, reluctantly, need to limit them. You could add your own items to the list.

✔

Item	Possible ways of limiting	Can eliminate	Can limit
Phone calls *Visitors dropping by* *Demands by family members*	*Ask people to call by phone or in person at specific times. Answer the phone but say you'll call back. Specify a time which is yours. Lock the door.*		
TV	*Limit it by type of programme, or time each day.*		
Socialising	*Only go out after 9pm, or only on set nights or days.*		
Operating by trial and error	*Plan ahead. Ask for advice from lecturers/friends.*		
Not able to contact people	*Leave messages. Write notes rather than make repeated calls. Say where you can be contacted.*		
Locating resources	*Ask the librarian or Learning Resources Department.*		
Putting things off	*Use this SkillPack.*		

NOTES

3.4.3 The working environment

Everyone has different ways of working which suit them best. Use the box below to assess your preferred working style.

What time of day do I study best?

How long can I concentrate before I need a break?

Where do I study best?

What circumstances help me study?

Do I work better under pressure?

Do I work better alone or with others?

3.4.4 Actions needed

- **What do you need to take action on?**
- **Which of the ideas in this SkillPack could you try out?**
- **What help do you need?**

For example, other SkillPacks might help. "Gathering and Using Information" (see Contents) looks at the efficient collection of information. "Coping with Pressure" (see Contents) looks at how to cope with a pressurised workload. Other sources of help include friends (how do they do things?), keeping a diary to monitor what you are trying to change, and guidance from lecturers.

Use the box below to set out where and what types of action you need to take.

In need of attention	Actions to take	Help needed

NOTES

3.5 REFERENCES AND BIBLIOGRAPHY

Libraries may have materials on this skill area. The following give examples:

Buzan, T. (1973), *Use your Head,* BBC Publications.

Hopson, B. and Scally, M. (1989), *Time Management: Conquer the Clock,* Lifeskills.

Jacques, D. (1990), *Studying at the Polytechnic,* Educational Methods Unit, Oxford Polytechnic.

Northedge, A. (1990), *The Good Study Guide,* Open University Press.

Stuart, R. R. (1989), *Managing Time,* The Pegasus Programme Understanding Industry Inst.

4
NOTE TAKING
by Sue Drew and Rosie Bingham

CONTENTS

Whilst studying you have to make notes: from lectures, seminars or tutorials; from books, written or computerised information; on visual images, like video, film, artwork; on your research methods (eg laboratory procedures and findings). You may consider that you have been taking notes for years perfectly adequately. Why should you reconsider this skill?

In universities and colleges you must look at information in more depth and more critically than at school. You will also be more reliant on effective notes than in the past and will simply be handling much more information. This means that your notes will need to be different.

It is easy to make notes, but difficult to make **good**, brief, accurate notes which summarise the essence of the information and which you can use and understand later.

We suggest you use this SkillPack:

- **at a point when you need to make notes**
- **in relation to the different sorts of notes you need to make – eg from lectures, for project work, from books etc.**

When you have completed it, you should be able to:

1 identify the purpose to which the notes will be put
2 identify main points
3 accurately identify the meaning of unfamiliar words, phrases and images
4 record images which provide a clear illustration of the points
5 accurately record sources of information
6 produce notes which are legible, well structured, and well organised for retrieval
7 use notes for the purpose for which they were intended.

You should be able to use the above elements of the skill on your course, from oral, visual, printed or computerised sources.

4.1 WHAT DO YOU DO AT THE MOMENT?

Do the following apply to you and your notes?

✔

Are your notes unselective, trying to cover everything?	
Are your notes difficult to follow later?	
Do you find it difficult to write notes, listen and understand in lectures/seminars/tutorials all at the same time?	
Do your notes highlight key points?	
Do your notes summarise main points?	
Do your notes clarify initial ideas?	

It can be useful to compare your lecture, assignment or lab notes with someone else's for a similar situation. You may find they are quite different even if you both were making notes on the same thing. Why? How?

Questions to ask in comparing notes might be:

- **In what ways are the notes different?**
- **How are the notes organised?**
- **Do you understand each other's notes?**
- **Why did you include some things and not others?**
- **Have they been rewritten or added to later?**
- **Will the notes still make sense in a month's time? (If another person doesn't understand your notes now it is likely you won't after a time lapse).**

How could I improve my notes?

NOTES

How could I improve my notes?

NOTES

4.2 THE PURPOSE OF YOUR NOTES

The reason for taking notes can determine what sort of notes you make. For example:

Is your purpose...	Possible implications	
for future revision?	Must be understandable after a long time lapse, contain all main points, be easy to follow.	
for an immediate assignment?	Must be accurate, may need to be detailed, able to be sorted to help structure the assignment. Not so important to be understandable after a long time lapse.	
for others to use?	Must be legible. Use abbreviations and words they will understand.	
to help concentration?	If they are not going to be used later, all that matters is helping you focus now.	
to record what happened?	Must be accurate, detailed.	
Add in any other purposes...		

4.3 SELECTING WHAT TO RECORD

What do you need to make notes on and what can be omitted?

If this crucial question is not addressed you may end up with patchy notes which don't make sense or with masses of irrelevant notes. It is rarely necessary, for example, to write down everything a lecturer says.

It helps to go back to your purpose. How much detail do you need for that purpose? What are the crucial aspects of the information?

Generally speaking, courses or programmes in universities and colleges aim for students to progress from initially providing descriptions of factual information towards identifying principles, concepts, arguments and being able to criticise and evaluate.

Being critical and evaluative means asking why information, concepts or arguments are as they are, eg:

- **On what assumptions are they based?**
- **Where does the information come from and might it be biased?**
- **What opposing views might there be?**
- **In what way might the information be inaccurate?**

It can help to think of information in three different categories.

Type of information	When important	Examples of questions to ask
Underlying principles, concepts, theories, lines of argument.	In universities and colleges this is very important. As you move into the final stages of a course it becomes crucial.	What are the ideas behind detailed, factual information? What are the crucial principles? If you had to explain a theory to a Martian, what would be its absolute essentials? What are the steps in a line of argument?
Detailed, factual information (includes details of recommended reading or sources to follow up).	As evidence for an argument, concept, principle, theory.	What is the argument/concept/ principle/theory which needs supporting? What evidence is needed to support it? Are there any essential steps (eg stages in a mathematical calculation) which must be included?
Your own questions, criticisms, opinions of the information.	This becomes even more important as you move into the final stages of a course.	Why is the information like that? Who says? On what assumptions is it based? What alternative views might there be? Is it accurate?

NOTES

You could take a particular source of information (eg a lecture, a book, a film) and make notes using the framework outlined on the previous page.

Principles, concepts, theories, arguments

Relevant detailed factual information

My own questions, criticisms etc

4.4 RECORDING THE INFORMATION

You need to consider how you wish to use the notes in order to decide how to record them. In what format would you find them helpful?

Long sentences are time consuming to write and read back. All that may be needed to reconstruct the idea are key words and phrases. Theories about how the brain works suggest that we remember by associating one idea with another, or by "accessing" information from the brain by use of trigger words or ideas (eg remembering a person's name by remembering where you met).

The following are common types of note taking:

4.4.1 Linear notes (do your notes look like these?)

Linear notes may be more effective if they:

- **contain key words and phrases**
- **use clear headings, subheadings, underlining, circles, boxes, diagrams, flow charts and colours**
- **have margins or are written on every other line so you can return to previous parts as the lecture or video progresses or you get further into the book or other source**
- **have margins for you to write your own questions, comments or criticisms (done so that in the future you do not mistake your own comments for those of a lecturer or author).**

4.4.2 Patterns

This method uses arrows and circles to connect the key words/phrases. It produces a spreading pattern in all directions rather than words which start at the top of the page and work down.

It may look messy but the content can be concise and quick to read. It is also easy and quick to redraw the pattern at a later stage to make it clearer.

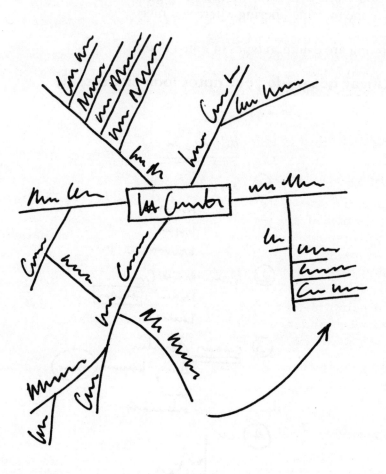

4.4.3 Visual information

It may be impossible to accurately record visual information verbally. How else could you record it? Possibilities include:

- **freehand sketches**
- **taking copies (but check the copyright situation with the library)**
- **taking down a good, accurate reference so you can find the visual again easily.**

4.4.4 Overall

You may want to combine linear and pattern styles in the same situation, using one piece of paper to draw patterns and another to note down factual information, lists etc. Whichever type of notes you use, it helps to write a few summarising lines to add to them.

For notes on class sessions it is useful to go over the notes that night or before the end of the week to check that they are understandable.

4.5 OBTAINING NOTES

4.5.1 Sharing note taking

You can spend more time listening if you share note taking, but check that those you work with have similar purposes for their notes and make understandable, legible notes. For example:

* **Sit in pairs in a lecture. One student should make notes on the first half, the other on the second half. Discuss the notes after the lecture.**
* **If you regularly work in groups, a different person each week can write notes and photocopy them for the rest.**
* **Book lists: students work in groups, each one being responsible for two or three books on the list, making notes on the relevant parts commenting on their usefulness and photocopying the notes for the others.**

4.5.2 Note taking in class

Ask lecturers or tutors to:

* **explain at the start of the class what will be covered in what order. The first and last 10 minutes of a lecture often summarise the main points**
* **break lectures into sections, of say 20 minutes, with pauses in between to help maintain attention**
* **indicate which aspects are really important**
* **allow students time to write notes at appropriate intervals**
* **explain points or terms you have not understood (if you ask, you may find that others haven't understood either)**
* **speak at a slower pace.**

If you are given lecture or tutorial handouts write additional notes during the class session in the margin or add your own pages.

4.5.3 Overall

Write notes in your own words. This helps you to understand and to remember.

It is helpful if your notes are dated and referenced – eg where they come from: lecture; video; book etc.

If you are making notes from text, include: title; date; author; place of publishing; and publisher. You could also record chapter headings and page numbers, especially if you need to find items again.

NOTES

4.6 USING NOTES

How usable are your notes? Would you describe them as:

✔

Short and concise?	
Easy to understand?	
Relevant?	
Well organised?	

4.6.1 Reviewing notes

Review notes soon after they have been made, highlighting things you do not understand and making them clearer. It is easier to act on misunderstandings or omissions while they are fresh in your mind.

How could you find out about things you don't understand? From other students? A Library Information Desk? Reference books? General or subject specific dictionaries? Encyclopaedias?

4.6.2 Retrieving notes

Will you be able to find your notes again easily? How will you store them? How will you retrieve the information?

Do you order notes by date order, alphabetically, numerically, by topic or subject? See the chapter on Gathering and Using Information in Part I for ideas.

Storage method	Possible advantages
Looseleaf in files	Can introduce new divisions, add extra material.
Concertina file/folders	Can introduce new divisions, add extra material.
Computerised database	Easy to edit.
Boxed card-file system	Good for an index or references, can be stored easily – eg in a card box index you can write on a card a topic and where you have stored it.
A notebook per topic	Keeps relevant material together.

4.7 REFERENCES AND BIBLIOGRAPHY

Libraries may have materials on this skill area. The following give examples:

Buzan, T. (1973), *Use your Head*, BBC Publications.

Gibbs, G. (1981), *Teaching Students to Learn*, Open University Press.

Habeshaw, S., Habeshaw, J. and Gibbs, G. (1987), *53 Interesting Ways of Helping your Students to Study*, Technical & Educational Services Ltd.

Jacques, D. (1990), *Studying at the Polytechnic*, Educational Methods Unit, Oxford Polytechnic.

National Extension College (1994), *Learning Skills Resource Bank: Notes for Tutors and Trainers*, NEC.

Northedge, A. (1990), *The Good Study Guide*, Open University Press.

Stuart, R. R. (1989), *Managing Time*, The Pegasus Programme Understanding Industry Inst.

NOTES

5
GATHERING AND USING INFORMATION

by Sue Drew, Aileen Wade and Andrew Walker

CONTENTS

Coursework requires you to find and effectively use good quality, relevant and up-to-date information. Your grades or marks will be strongly influenced by your skills in this area.

We also live in an information society, and you will need information skills in most professions.

In this Pack, "information" refers to:

• written material
• numerical material
• computerised material
• audio-visual material – eg videos, interactive videos, films, multimedia packages
• visual materials – eg photographs, diagrams and graphs, or works of art.

We suggest you use this SkillPack:

• **when you need to gather information for a course activity or assignment**
• **before you begin to gather any information**
• **then whilst gathering information.**

When you have completed it, you should be able to

1 find sources of information relevant to, and sufficient for, the purpose and audience
2 use effective reading and observing strategies – eg skimming, scanning, in depth reading or viewing
3 identify the meaning of subject-specific terminology as used in the programme units studied
4 identify the main points or issues of relevance to the topic
5 accurately record sources of information

You should be able to use the above elements of the skill on your course, with support or clarification from libraries, reference books, tutors and other students.

5.1 WHAT IS YOUR PURPOSE?

To stay focused, it is important to be clear about what information you need, why and who you need it for. Section 5.1.4 below contains a box for you to summarise your responses to Sections 5.1.1, 5.1.2 and 5.1.3.

5.1.1 Analysing the task

Any information-seeking (eg how to get from A to B) starts with research questions (eg what buses or trains go from A to B, when and at what cost?). A course task or assignment may not be phrased as a question but it helps to identify what you need to ask to be able to complete it.

If you are uncertain about what is needed, ask your lecturer or tutor, so that you avoid completing a task only to discover you have misunderstood it.

Two examples are given below:

"Discuss the transport policy of the City of Sheffield"	"Develop a database on transport in Sheffield"
• *What is the transport policy?* • *Why was it developed?* • *What are the costs and benefits?* • *What is right or wrong with it?*	• *Who would want to use the database?* • *How would they access the database?* • *What should the database contain?*

5.1.2 Why do you want the information? Who is it for?

Why you want the information and for whom influences the amount and depth of information needed as well as the focus.

For example:

Why discuss transport policy?	Who is the discussion for?
• *to persuade others that different transport is needed* • *to illustrate the main issues in developing transport policies* • *to provide practice at discussing an issue from differing perspectives and argue a point*	• *your lecturer – to see how much you understand; how well you use information; to assess your skills* • *your seminar group – to share information and understanding* • *the City Council – to help it make decisions*

Why develop a transport database?	Who is the database for?
• *to provide information about transport provision* • *to give practice in creating databases* • *to highlight the important issues in creating databases*	• *your lecturer – to see how much you understand; how you can use information; to assess your skills* • *the public – to identify what transport they can use*

5.1.3 When do you need it by?

How much time you have can influence how you go about collecting information, and how much you can gather. For example, if you only have a week you have no time to write off for information. Similarly if you want a book which another student has on loan or the material is not available at your university or college library and needs to be obtained from elsewhere, you may have to wait several days or even a few weeks.

This implies planning ahead. You may find it helpful to refer to "Organising Yourself and Your Time" (see Contents).

5.1.4 Summary

We suggest you complete the following for your assignment or course activity.

What questions do you need to answer?	Why?	For whom?	By when?

NOTES

5.2 UNDERSTANDING THE TERMINOLOGY

Terminology may be subject-specific, and new to you. It helps to:

- **identify words you don't understand**
- **use general dictionaries and a thesaurus (which gives a range of words with the same or similar meaning)**
- **use specialist dictionaries – eg accounting, business, medical dictionaries**
- **use glossaries in books**
- **use encyclopedias**
- **ask your lecturer/tutor**
- **ask at a Library Information Desk.**

5.3 HOW WILL YOU RECORD THE INFORMATION?

5.3.1 Plagiarism

Plagiarism is copying someone else's words or work and using it in your own work without acknowledging it. Whilst it is very important to quote from, or summarise, published work which is correctly referenced, it is not acceptable to plagiarise. Assessors may think you are trying to pass off somebody else's work as your own.

5.3.2 Recording information

You need to record information in such a way that:

- **it matches the way you can use it in whatever format you want to present it (eg in a written report, on disk)**
- **you can find it and use it again in the future if you need to**
- **you know where it came from (not only should should you reference all sources properly in assignments, but you also may need to find them again)**
- **you will not have to return to the same source again to recheck details**
- **it suits your own way of working.**

Having a well organised system will save you time. You may find it helpful to refer to "Note Taking" (see Contents).

How do you record information now?

In a notebook
In a looseleaf folder with file dividers
On a single side of paper to help in ordering your notes
On cards
On a computer database
In piles on the floor
On scraps of paper
Others (please specify)

How do you classify information so that you can find it?

By subject   *eg transport*

By topic   *eg trains*

By author   *eg Gunston, B.*

By cross references   *eg you file alphabetically by one set of topics but*
                              also have index cards showing which of those files
                              also contain other topics. For example:

Main file	Cross reference index
Trains	*Chassis*
Buses	*Engines*
Lorries	*Safety*

In no particular way (just rifle through the piles)

This is what an index card might look like.

TOPIC -	TRANSPORT
AUTHOR -	GUNSTON B. (1976) <u>LORRIES, BUSES AND TRAINS</u> MACMILLAN
WHERE LOCATED -	CITY CAMPUS LIBRARY
LIBRARY REFERENCE NO.	629.2GU

Street - railroads
Trucks
Buses

NOTES

5.3.3 Referencing

Not only should you always acknowledge any thoughts, ideas and information which are not your own, you should also use a standard form of referencing to provide all the relevant information, should anyone else wish to look up the work.

This means that you need to keep accurate records of references during your information gathering to avoid having to go back and recheck them.

Referring to an item in your text is known as citing. You then need a list of references at the end of your work to indicate where that citation can be found.
Examples:

Citations

There are two universally accepted methods. You can use either, but keep to the same one in one piece of work. This chapter uses the Harvard system.

Harvard system
Give the author's name and the date of publication in brackets,
eg "Gibbs (1992) believes students should be active."
Direct quotations should also include the page number.
eg "Gibbs (1992, p11) states that 'students need to be active ...' "

Numeric system
Number your references as they appear in the text and then use the same number each time you refer to it,
eg "In a recent report (26) it was stated that 'students need to be active...' "

Referencing

At the end of an assignment, all works referred to should be listed. If using the Harvard system list them alphabetically by surname (last name); if using the numeric system list them by number. In either case you need the following information:

Book
• **name of author/editor, with initials**
• **date of publication, in brackets**
• **book title, including any other information underlined**
• **the publisher's name**
• **some lecturers may require the place of publication.**

eg *Gibbs, G. (1992), <u>Improving the Quality of Student Learning</u>, Technical and Educational Services, Bristol.*

Media (eg video)
• **author**
• **date of publication**
• **format and length**
• **accompanying material**

eg *Main, A. (1987), <u>Study Patterns: Introductory Programme Plus Units 1-4</u>, 3rd ed., Audio Visual Services, University of Strathclyde: Guild Sound and Vision, VHS video cassette – 3 hrs and booklet.*

Article
• **name of author(s), with initials**
• **date of publication, in brackets**
• **title of article**
• **name of journal, underlined**
• **volume, number and pages**

eg *Rainer, R. and Reimann, P. (1989), "The bipolarity of personal constructs", <u>International Journal of Personal Construct Theory</u>, vol. 3 (2), pp149-165.*

5.4 WHERE MIGHT YOU FIND THE INFORMATION?

5.4.1 What location?

The starting point is your university or college library which should have an Information Desk. Subject librarians and other specialists will also give advice and guidance.

Where else might you try? Consider who might have an interest in the topic and want to keep information on this area. For instance, for information on transport providers, you could approach railway companies, bus companies etc, environmental groups and trades unions.

Libraries have directories listing addresses of such organisations.

5.4.2 How might the information be organised?

Being aware of how information can be organised may help in finding it. For example, libraries give each item a number and the items are then organised in numerical order based on decisions the librarian makes, eg about what subject it belongs to. Possible ways of organising information include:

- **by author**
- **by publication type (eg journal)**
- **by title**
- **by language**
- **by subject**
- **by date**
- **by key word** – eg in the example "Transport policies in Sheffield" either "transport" or "Sheffield" might be the key word.

In a library you can "search" for an item by using any of these starting points and you will then find the number indicating where the item is stored.

5.4.3 How do you know you have found all the possible information?

There are a number of possible reasons for being unable to find information. You need to know which one applies, so that you know what to do about it.

Reason	Implications
People make decisions about how to organise information and they may have looked at it from an angle which is different from yours.	Try looking for it under other related subjects. Try identifying other possible key words. Ask at a Library Information Desk.
The information might not exist.	Finding this out may mean you have to collect information from scratch yourself. Researchers always start by looking for what information already exists to avoid duplicating it.
The information might exist, but not be available – eg it might be confidential.	This might be very useful to find out, especially if you could identify reasons for this.

If in doubt, ask at a Library Information Desk.

5.5 USING INFORMATION

5.5.1 Covering all the information

You may have a lot of information to consider. New technology means much more material can be found or accessed. How will you cover it all? There are three levels of helpful strategies. Use the first to identify what you need to look at in the second, and the second to see what you need to look at in the third.

Level	Strategy	What I currently do	What I could try
Superficial	Skimming/scanning. Don't read every word, or look at every detail, instead look at • titles • contents pages • headings • overall image (for visual items).		
Refined	Read introductions. Read first and last lines of paragraphs. Look at charts/diagrams. Look for key words.		
Detailed/ in-depth	Careful, thoughtful reading or observation to understand all aspects.		

NOTES

5.5.2 Knowing when you have enough information

The following checklists may help.

✔

Has the information started repeating itself?	
Have you covered the core material? (You may need guidance from the lecturer)	
Have you answered your research questions?	
Is the information peripheral, not relevant to the research questions, superfluous?	
Does the information offer anything new?	

✔

I can't digest any more.	
I don't have any time to use any more.	
I have too much paper or my storage space (eg physical or on disk) is full.	

5.5.3 Answering your research questions

You are unlikely to find information in exactly the right form to complete a task. For example, if you are required to compare theories or authors or materials you will be unlikely to find a text which does it for you. You need to find the original materials and compare them for yourself.

Tasks set at university or college assume that you need to gather information from various sources and then make sense of it.

5.6 REFERENCES AND BIBLIOGRAPHY

Libraries may have materials on this skill area. The following give examples:

Bell, J. (1987), *Doing Your Own Research Project: A Guide for First-time Researchers in Education and Social Science*, Open University Press.

Northedge, A. (1990), *The Good Study Guide*, Open University Press.

Pauk, W. (1989), *How to Study in College*, (4th edn), Houghton Mifflin.

Videos

Secrets of Study (interactive video) (1989), Mast Learning Systems.

NOTES

6
ESSAY WRITING
by Theresa Lillis

CONTENTS

The word "essay" originally meant a first attempt or practice, but it now means a piece of writing on a specific subject. Writing an essay involves responding to a question or title set by a tutor and takes the form of an argument, leading the reader from the title at the beginning to a final conclusion.

Why is it important to write essays well?
Essays continue to be an important means of assessment.

Writing helps to clarify your ideas about a topic, form arguments and identify what is relevant, and therefore helps you learn. You are more likely to remember something you have written than something you have read.

The requirements for essays vary according to subject and individual tutors, so you should ask lecturers/tutors for details of assessment criteria. However, there are requirements common to all disciplines. This SkillPack focuses on the common requirements and aims to help you produce a successful essay.

We suggest you use this SkillPack:

- **to consider what writing an essay involves**
- **to evaluate your current essay writing skills**
- **to improve your essay writing skills.**

When you have completed it, you should be able to:

1. present the essay in a clearly structured form, appropriate for the purpose and audience
2. produce a sequenced argument, reflected in the structure of the essay
3. plan strategies for producing the essay
4. act on your understanding of the explicit and implicit tasks in the title
5. gather, sort and present evidence to substantiate a case, using appropriate referencing techniques
6. follow standard conventions for grammar, spelling and punctuation
7. use appropriate conventions of academic presentation – eg referencing
8. comply with the regulations on plagiarism
9. proofread, edit and review the work
10. use feedback to improve performance.

You should be able to use this skill on your course with guidance from your tutors.

6.1 WHAT DOES WRITING A SUCCESSFUL ESSAY INVOLVE?

Writing an essay involves various activities. There is no right way to get from start to finish and writers, beginners or experienced, use different strategies, but the diagram below summarises processes which seem to be essential.

```
                    ┌─────────────────┐
                    │  Choosing a     │
                    │ question/title  │
                    └─────────────────┘
                    ┌─────────────────┐
                    │  Analysing a    │
                    │   question      │
                    └─────────────────┘
  ┌──────────────────┐         ┌──────────────────────┐
  │ Gathering relevant│        │ Generating ideas/plans│
  │   information     │        │   – brainstorming     │
  └──────────────────┘         └──────────────────────┘
  ┌──────────────────┐         ┌──────────────────────┐
  │ Clarifying what   │        │  Talking to others –  │
  │ finished essay    │        │   tutors, friends     │
  │ should look like  │        └──────────────────────┘
  └──────────────────┘              ┌──────────┐
      ┌──────────┐                  │ Drafting │
      │ Focus on │                  └──────────┘
      │ revising │              ┌──────────────┐
      └──────────┘              │  Rereading   │
                                │   drafts     │
            ┌──────────────────┐└──────────────┘
            │ Producing the    │
            │ finished essay   │
            └──────────────────┘
```

Factors to consider:

- **Time**
- **Current skills**

6.2 USING THIS SKILLPACK

6.2.1 Evaluate your current skills

We suggest you use the list below to consider your current essay writing skills and to identify where you need further guidance.

Do you know how to...	✔
find out what is expected?	
get started?	
gather information?	
express your ideas clearly?	
sequence an argument?	
support your argument?	
reference your sources?	
produce a clear structure?	
revise your drafts?	
edit your drafts?	
present your essay appropriately?	
use feedback from your tutors?	

All of these topics are covered in this SkillPack.

6.2.2 How to use this SkillPack

It will help to work through this SkillPack while you are preparing an essay, especially if it is the first essay you have written in a long time or if you feel unsure about it.

If you feel generally confident about essay writing, turn to the pages which focus on areas of specific interest to you.

6.3 FINDING OUT WHAT IS EXPECTED

Be clear about your task. Before you begin, establish what is expected in terms of the content, length and form of the essay. This can depend on subject, course and individual lecturers, so ask your tutor what s/he expects.

6.3.1 Understanding the question: explicit demands

It sounds obvious, but your essay must answer the question. Work out the explicit demands – ie what the question is obviously about. One way of doing this is to identify the following:

- **topic:** what the question is generally about
- **focus:** the specific aspect of the topic you will concentrate on
- **instructions:** what the tutor wants you to do.

If there are concepts/words in the question that you do not understand, ask your tutor. Use the following to analyse your essay question.

Essay Question	Example: *Discuss the principal methods of controlling noise at work*	Your Question:
Topic	*Noise at work*	
Focus	*Principal methods of controlling*	
Instruction	*Discuss*	

(Based on Hamp-Lyons, 1987:140)

What common instruction words in essay questions usually mean	
Analyse	Break a question/issue into its component parts and explain how they relate to one another.
Assess	Estimate the importance or value of something.
Compare	Examine similarities and differences.
Contrast	Concentrate on the differences.
Criticise	Point out the faults, limitations and usefulness of the subject in question.
Define	Explain the precise meaning of something.
Describe	Give a detailed account of a topic.
Discuss	Explain the meaning of something and present a logical argument exploring it.
Evaluate	Weigh up the importance, success or value of something, using evidence to support your view.
Examine	Give a detailed account of something, questioning and exploring relevant issues.
Explain	Give a precise account of something, with reasons for why or how it is as it is.
Illustrate	Use examples from a range of sources to demonstrate the subject of the essay. This may include written description of visual materials – eg diagrams, photographs.
Justify or prove	Make a case for a particular perspective. Establish the truth of something through supporting evidence or logical reasoning.
Review	Examine how a topic has been studied and comment on the value and limitations of its treatment.
Literature review	Survey the literature written on a subject, outlining key themes, points of discussion and gaps.
State	Write the main points relating to the subject.
Summarise	Give the main points of something.
To what extent?	Similar to evaluate: explore the case for and against a claim.

6.3.2 Understanding the question: implicit demands

I felt pretty satisfied with my essay. I thought I'd get a brilliant mark for it. So I was really put off when I saw the tutor's comments. I just thought it was what the essay title said: "What limits a person's ability to do two things at once?" Not why, or how it was done. What I did I thought was very relevant, but the tutor wanted "how" and "why" factors, and I didn't quite answer that. (Taken from Hounsell and Murray, 1992: 24).

It is important to be aware of *implicit* (the less obvious) expectations in essay questions. For example:

- Look **beyond** the explicit demands of the question. Acting on key words may not be enough.
- At college or university, whatever the essay title, you are expected not only to describe but also to **analyse** a topic.

Why has the question been set? Is it for you to demonstrate:

- **specific subject knowledge** – are you expected to use lectures/seminars, course or wider reading, certain writers?
- **personal experience** – are you expected to use personal experience or not?
- **understanding of theory and practice** – should you draw on a combination of these?
- **communication skills** – will you be assessed on how you use language, organise material, present your argument?

If you are unsure about any implicit expectations, ask your tutor.

	Example: Discuss the principal methods of controlling noise at work	The implicit demands of <u>your</u> essay question...?
Implicit demands?	*Question whether/why noise should be controlled. Need to:* • *analyse definitions of noise* • *describe principal methods of controlling noise.* • *examine the advantages/ disadvantages of the methods.*	
Clarification needed?	*Are there particular sources I need to use?* *Were key points highlighted/explored in lectures, seminars?* *What is the lecturer's view on this issue? What's my view?*	

NOTES

6.4 GETTING STARTED

Writing can be approached in many ways. Different strategies work for different people. Any of the following could be a starting point.

6.4.1 Write a plan

Think of a plan as flexible, to be altered, rewritten or thrown out as your writing progresses. Professional writers produce many plans as their writing takes shape and it is only one of a range of activities they use. The following questions may help:

- **What are the main issues/ideas to cover?**
- **How will you cover the ideas? Will you draw on particular writers, practice, personal experience?**
- **What will the main points be?**
- **What examples, references, quotes will be useful?**
- **What conclusions will you reach (eg firm, cautious)?**
- **Are there any theoretical/practical implications of your conclusions?**

6.4.2 Make a list/brainstorm

Write down ideas and words, as a list on one piece of paper or on separate pieces. This shows how many ideas you have and if you need to read, talk or listen to generate more. Using a word processor means you can easily re-order your list of ideas.

6.4.3 Write a mind map

After writing down the ideas, try to link them, as in the example below.

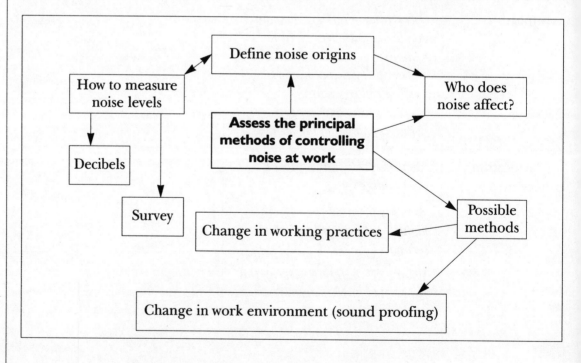

6.4.4 Talk

Talking to others (tutor, friends) helps to clarify ideas and test them out.

6.4.5 Write

It can help to write a draft straight off. Write on one side of a page so that you can reorder it by cutting and pasting. If you use a word processor, use the cut and paste functions.

Try some of the above ideas and note how useful they were.

Method	Comments

NOTES

6.5 GATHERING INFORMATION

It helps to list the information needed for your essay and where you might find it.
This may change as your ideas develop.

Information needed to answer your question	The source of information you already have – eg the book, journal, section of lecture notes	Possible source/ location of further information

For further advice see "Gathering and Using Information" (see Contents).

6.5.1 Academic conventions: abbreviations

When reading for your essay, you may come across the following terms. You may also be expected to use them in your writing. Ask your tutor if you are not sure about what is expected in your subject area.

NOTES

c. (circa)	about a certain date (as in "c. 1901")
ch., chs (or chap., chaps)	chapter(s)
ed., eds	editor(s)
edn	edition
e.g. (exempla gratia)	for example
et al. (et alia)	"and others" (used when a book has several authors, as in "P. March et al.")
et seq (et sequentes)	"and following" (as in "pp. 64 et seq.")
f., ff.	"and the following" (to refer to page numbers as in "pp. 30 ff.")
ibid. (ibidem)	"in the same work" (as previously cited)
i.e. (id est)	that is/that is to say
loc. cit. (loco citato)	"in the same place (already) cited" (that is, in the same passage referred to in a recent reference note)
ms, mss	manuscript(s)
n., nn.	note(s) (as "p. 56, n. 3" or "p. 56 n.")
n.d.	no date (of publications)
n.p.	no place (of publication)
op. cit. (opere citato)	in the work cited (used with a page number)
p., pp.	page(s)
passim	"throughout the work" (rather than on specific pages)
rev.	revised (by), reviser
[sic]	"thus so" (to guarantee exact quotation when the reader might doubt this)
trans., tr.	translator, -ion, -ed
v., vv.	verse
viz. (videlicet)	"namely", "in other words" (usually after words or statements, about to be elaborated)
vols., vols.	volume(s)

Punctuation conventions may vary from publisher to publisher. For instance, in this series of SkillPacks, eg is written without punctuation.

6.6 WRITING YOUR ESSAY

6.6.1 Drafting

How do I know what I think until I see what I say? (E. M. Forster in Murray, 1982:86)

However you generate ideas, only by writing will you actually learn to write. At times, you will need to force yourself to write even if you are unsure about what to say. Writing not only helps you to clarify your ideas but to discover them.

It may help to start by writing in complete sentences about anything relevant to your essay – eg part of your introduction, an idea to explore or a summary of key facts.

You need to continually revise and edit your work. Some writers do this as they go along, others leave it until they have completed a draft (see Sections 6.7 and 6.8). You will need at least one draft before your final version and possibly several.

6.6.2 Expressing ideas clearly

Tutors expect you to express your ideas in your own words but also to use terminology relevant to the subject. The following will help you to think about your writing.

Focus	Suggestions	What you can do in your first draft
Words and phrases	Use words in a way which demonstrates you understand them. When first referring to an idea/concept give the reader enough information to understand it. Don't assume that your reader knows.	Underline words/phrases you are unsure of. Use a dictionary, lecture notes and texts to check that you are using them correctly. If you use a thesaurus to find new words, check their meaning in the dictionary.
Sentences	If sentences are too short, the ideas may seem fragmented. If they are too long, they may be difficult to follow. If you find writing difficult or if English is your second language, short sentences may help you avoid grammatical mistakes.	Read your sentences aloud, to help you to make sure they make sense. Get a friend to read any you're unsure about, to see if s/he understands what you are saying.
Paragraphs	Keep to one main idea per paragraph. Ensure the idea is explicitly stated and explained.	Underline the main idea in each paragraph. If there is more than one idea, is an extra paragraph needed or are there irrelevancies you can cut?
Linking paragraphs	Link ideas across paragraphs so your argument flows. "Also", "moreover", "in addition" show that you are continuing in the same direction; "whereas", "nevertheless", "however", "on the other hand" to show that you are changing direction.	Underline words and phrases which show how you have linked paragraphs. Get a friend to read several paragraphs and ask her/him whether they can see how they relate.

6.6.3 Developing an argument: sequencing

Argument is an essential feature of essays. "Argument" may mean putting forward a perspective supported by evidence – ie arguing a particular case. With essays the word is used more generally to mean **the development of a clear line of thought**. There is no one way to present ideas and thoughts but it is essential to organise them into a sequence meaningful to the reader.

Below are outlines of successful arguments in two student essays. Read the examples and then summarise the key moves in the development of **your** argument in **your** essay – ie the sequence of your main points and how they link together. You may only be able to outline part of your argument, but you can return to this as your essay develops.

Examples of key moves (see above) in developing an argument in two sample essays.

Example 1

Essay title/question
Analyse the role of non-verbal communication within the communication process, noting how it can work in isolation and in combination with other forms of communication.

What the writer does in a sequence of key moves
Defines terms and definitions of non-verbal communication.
Describes non-verbal communication in isolation, using information from reading.
Describes non-verbal communication in combination with other sorts of communication, using information from reading.
Highlights limitations and complexities.
Summarises key points in relation to the essay question.

NOTES

NOTES

Example 2

Essay title/question
Discuss the social responsibilities of software engineers.

What the writer does in a sequence of key moves
Makes a claim – software engineers have social responsibilities.
Defines terms – social/responsibility. Uses specific and general information to put definitions into context.
Introduces complicating factor – responsibilities to employer v. public. Uses specific example to put into context.
Suggests possible solution to problem posed.
Uses specific information from other sources to support proposed solution. Conclusion: takes particular position – need for compromise.

Your essay title/question

The sequence of your key moves

6.6.4 Supporting your argument

You should provide evidence for your argument, using written text or visuals such as graphs, tables and illustrations as appropriate. Certain types of evidence are preferred in some subjects, and it helps to discuss this with your tutor.

✔

How could you support different points in your argument?	If using in your essay
Logical reasoning *Example* *There are several possible explanations why the motivation and academic performance of students change during their three years at college. In the first year, students mature, adapt to a new learning environment and reveal new interests and talents which may move them away from previous skills and pursuits (Sharp, 1994:142).*	
Citing authorities *Example* *Whittle et al. (1995) have shown that the hepatitis B vaccination is effective in the long term.*	
Drawing on findings of research/experiment carried out by you or others (also known as empirical evidence). *Example* *The graph below shows the usage of SkillPacks at Sheffield Hallam University.* Starter Packs Used at Sheffield Hallam University © *Drew & Bingham (1996)*	
Drawing on personal life experience *Example* *From my perspective as Head of Adult and Community Education at the college, with previous experience at a large urban community college, I believe that growth can only be sustained by developing extensive outreach networks (Thorn 1995:243).*	

NOTES

6.6.5 Acknowledging sources and referencing

While you work, record the works you use, so that you can acknowledge them in your essay. If you do not give full references to them, you may be accused of plagiarism (copying). You can be failed for plagiarising the work of authors or fellow students. Plagiarism also stops you from articulating ideas in ways meaningful to you and may prevent learning.

Citing or referencing within the essay
Find out which of the different ways of citing/referencing is used in your subject. The Harvard system is used here.

For guidance on gathering information see "Gathering and Using Information" (see Contents).

You need to give a citation or reference when you...	Example	Have you done this?
use quotations. For quotations use double quotation marks " " and/or a different font (type face). Give the publication date and page number on which the quote appeared.	Steve Jones points out that *"the new fluidity of DNA alarms geneticists as it violates the idea of gene as particle"* (1993:85).	
summarise/explain the ideas of other writers. For a general comment then give the surname of the author(s) and year of publication.	*Experiential learning provides opportunities for students to develop interpersonal skills, self-awareness, reflection, insight and problem-solving skills (Raichura, 1987 and Burnard, 1989).*	
refer to a specific idea or piece of information. Also give the page number.	*Women make up 9 per cent of the total number of people with Aids in the US (Watney, 1991:2).*	
mention the writer in your text. Do not give the name again in brackets.	*Hallam and Marshment (1995) have critically explored the adaptation of Winterson's novel for television.*	
NOTE: If you use someone's ideas as described by another writer rather than in the original text, you need to point this out.	*Poplack describes three types of code switching (in Romaine, 1989:113)*	

Final references

NOTES

At the end of your essay, list the works to which you have referred. Each book reference should include the following in this order:
- **surname, initial**
- **year of publication**
- **title**
- **publisher**
- **place of publication if required**

For each article reference, you need:

- **the article's title**
- **the journal's title**
- **the volume and issue number**
- **the page number(s)**

Titles of books and journals should be underlined or in italics if using a word processor.

The list should be in alphabetical order according to surname.

6.6.6 References relating to Section 6.6.5 of this SkillPack

Burnard, P. (1989), "Experiential learning and androgogy – negotiated learning in nurse education: a critical appraisal", *Nurse Education Today*, **9** (5), pp.300-306.

Hallam, J. and Marshment, M. (1995), "Training experience: case studies in the reception of 'Oranges are Not the Only Fruit'", *Screen*, **36** (1), pp.1-16.

Jones, S. (1993), *The Language of the Genes*, Flamingo.

Raichura, L. (1987), "Learning by doing", *Nursing Times*, **83** (13), pp.59-61.

Romaine, S. (1989), *Bilingualism*, Basil Blackwell.

Thorn, L. (1995), "Using outreach in a rural tertiary college", *Adults Learning* **6** (8), pp.243-6.

Watney, S. (1991), "Aids: the second decade: risk research and modernity", Aggleton, P., Hart, P. and Davies, P. (eds), *Aids Responses, Interventions and Care*, Falmer Press.

Young, A. (1995), "Peer and parental pressure within the sociolinguistic environment: an Anglo-French comparative study of teenage foreign language learners", *Language in a Changing Europe*, BAAL.

Have you checked your final references?
After reading the list above, make any necessary alterations.

6.6.7 Checking overall structure

When you have completed your draft, check your structure. ✔

Key points		Done
Introduction	Define your topic, state the main issues to be covered and how you will deal with them.	
Main body of essay	Develop your argument, using evidence and analysis to support your statements. Present your ideas one at a time in a logical sequence which enables the reader to follow your line of thought.	
Conclusion	Sum up your ideas and highlight key points made in the main part of your essay. State your conclusions, relating them to the essay title. You can suggest implications for further research or exploration.	
References	List all the works referred to in your essay (see Section 6.6.5).	

6.7 REVISING YOUR ESSAY

Revising here means focusing on your meaning. Some people revise as they write, others when they have produced a fairly long draft, others do both. ✔

Ask yourself...	What you can do	Further work needed
Does it make sense to you?	Read it aloud at a normal speed	
Will it make sense to the reader?	Ask somebody to read it. Tell them what you want them to look for – eg can they identify the key ideas?	
Have you said all you wanted to? Have you missed anything out? Is it all relevant?	Read it through. Check with your rough drafts, outlines, brainstorms, notes.	
Are your ideas in a logical order?	Check if: • the main ideas in each paragraph are clearly expressed. Are there too many? • you have linked ideas across paragraphs • you have presented a clear line of thought, from the introduction to the conclusion.	
Is your supporting evidence correct, specific and detailed?	Check details you are unsure of, using lecture notes, relevant books, articles.	

6.8 EDITING YOUR ESSAY

Editing is used here to mean examining the language and presentation in your essay. These may have an important bearing on your grade.

Focus on...	Checked ✔	Notes of errors for future action
Spelling • specialist terminology • spelling in general. Use a spellchecker if working on a word processor. Spellcheckers do not examine spelling in context, so look for words which sound the same but are spelled differently – eg *principle/principal, practice/practise, there/their, two/to/too, assent/ascent.*		
Grammar Look for grammatical mistakes (standard corrections are in italics). Common errors are: • Not putting a finite verb in each sentence: eg "Going down the stairs two at a time." is not a sentence. *"He was going down the stairs two at a time."* • Lack of pronoun agreement in sentences: eg "**The tutor** has a responsibility to **their** *(his/her)* students". • Unclear use of pronouns for reference: eg "**This** is a major problem". It may not be clear what **this** refers to. • Inconsistent use of tenses: eg "Pupils must have confidence in their ability before they **could** *(can)* actually use foreign languages". • Unclear sentence boundaries: eg "If in the software industry things get patched up and without social responsibilities in the event such patching up could lead to damage it would be ignored". An alternative might be *"A job which is badly carried out in the software industry might lead to damage. If a software engineer has no sense of social responsibility, such damage could go unnoticed."* • Influence of speech on writing: eg "He could **of** *(have)* examined the situation more carefully".		

NOTES

NOTES

Focus on...	Checked ✔	Notes of errors for future action
Apostrophe "s" This causes problems but the rules of use are as follows: • **There is no apostrophe in a plural** (more than one): eg books, pencils. • **There is an apostrophe before the "s" in abbreviations of the verb is/has:** eg "she's (is) a teacher; she's (has) had an operation". The ' indicates that something is missing. • **There is an apostrophe before the "s" in singular possession and after the "s" in plural possession:** *"The student's (one student) essay was good. The students' (more than one student) essays were good".*		
Punctuation Break up very long sentences, eg with commas. There are no definite rules but possibilities include using commas: before a "joining" word like "but"; to separate out part of a sentence which is an aside. Check that quotations have quotation marks around them. Check that lists are punctuated: eg *"There is a range of methods of transport: buses; trains; planes; cars".* Check that questions end with a question mark instead of a full stop.		
Presentation Ask yourself: • Is it legible? • Have you included the essay title, your name and title of the course? • Are you expected to use a word processor? • Have you followed conventions laid down by your tutor/course/programme? • Have you used visuals effectively and appropriately (eg tables, graphs, illustrations)?		

6.9 USING FEEDBACK ON YOUR ESSAY

Feedback from tutors is often in the form of a written comment on your essay. They may discuss their comments with you. Feedback can improve future essays.

When you get feedback from your tutor:

- **Read or listen to the comments carefully.**
- **Check that you understand the comments. If you aren't sure, ask.**
- **Discuss with your tutor areas on which to concentrate for your next essay.**
- **Categorise the comments made. For example, are there many comments on your referencing, or on the development of your argument? This tells you what to improve next time.**
- **Reread your feedback and any notes you make before your next essay.**
- **Produce an action plan based on feedback and on your views of what needs improving.**

Aspects of essay	Improvement needed	Action to be taken in next essay
Understanding and responding precisely to the question		
Expressing ideas clearly: • words appropriately used • key ideas in paragraphs • linking across paragraphs		
Developing argument		
Supporting argument		
Referencing sources		
Spelling		
Punctuation		
Grammar		
Presentation		

6.10 EXAMPLES OF ASSESSMENT SHEETS

An Assignment Attachment

Energy and Life Systems

Student's Name	Assignment Grade

Itemised Rating Scale

Structure

Essay relevant to topic	☐☐☐☐	Essay has little relevance
Topic covered in depth	☐☐☐☐	Superficial treatment of topic

Argument

Accurate presentation of evidence	☐☐☐☐	Much evidence inaccurate or questionable
Logically developed argument	☐☐☐☐	Essay rambles and lacks continuity
Original and creative thought	☐☐☐☐	Little evidence of originality

Style

Fluent piece of writing	☐☐☐☐	Clumsily written
Succinct writing	☐☐☐☐	Unnecessarily repetitive

Presentation

Legible and well set out work	☐☐☐☐	Untidy and difficult to read
Reasonable length	☐☐☐☐	Over/under length

Sources

Adequate acknowledgement of sources	☐☐☐☐	Inadequate acknowledgement of sources
Correct citation of references	☐☐☐☐	Incorrect referencing

Mechanics

Grammatical sentences	☐☐☐☐	Several ungrammatical sentences
Correct spelling throughout	☐☐☐☐	Much incorrect spelling
Effective use of figures and tables	☐☐☐☐	Figures and tables add little to argument
Correct use of units and quantities	☐☐☐☐	Some units incorrect

(Taken from Hounsell and Murray (1992, p40))

BA English Studies: Literature Assignment

Student:

Unit:

Brief Title:

Please tick the boxes below

1 = Fail   2 = Weak   3 = Average   4 = Good   5 = Excellent

		1	2	3	4	5
Assignment's relevance to title and nature and scope of the work as stated in your introduction	Student Tutor					
Structure/Organisation	Student Tutor					
Understanding and use of relevant critical terms and concepts	Student Tutor					
Originality of interpretation	Student Tutor					
Persuasiveness of interpretation	Student Tutor					
Prose style	Student Tutor					
Use of appropriate close textural reference	Student Tutor					
Understanding and use of relevant contexts (historical, social, generic etc.)	Student Tutor					
Appropriate use and proper acknowledgement of secondary sources	Student Tutor					
Technical accuracy (spelling, grammar etc.)	Student Tutor					
Presentation (neatness, legibility)	Student Tutor					

NOTES

Please give the assignment a mark

0 - 39	Fail	Student's Estimate	%
40 - 49	3rd	Tutor's Estimate	%
50 - 59	2.2		
60 - 69	2.1		
70 +	1st		

(From Dave Hurry, School of Cultural Studies, Sheffield Hallam University)

NOTES

6.11 REFERENCES AND WRITING AIDS

Hamp-Lyons, L. and Heasley, B. (1987), *Study Writing. A Course in Written English for Academic and Professional Purposes,* Cambridge University Press.

Hounsell, D. and Murray, R. (1992), "Essay writing for active learning"; *Effective Learning and Teaching in Higher Education,* CVCP Universities Staff Development and Training Unit.

Murray, D. (1982), "Learning by teaching", *Selected Articles on Writing and Teaching,* Heinemann.

Pearson, R. A. and Phelps, T. (1993), *Academic Vocabulary and Argument,* PAVIC Publications.

Writing aids

To help with spelling

Allen, R. E. (1986) *The Oxford Spelling Dictionary,* Oxford University Press.

Good self-assessment exercises on use of language

Collinson, D., Kirkup, G., Kyd, R., and Slocombe, L. (1992), *Plain English* (2nd edn) Oxford University Press.

Grammar for ESL/EFL students

Murphy, R. (1994), *English Grammar in Use* (2nd edn.) A self-study reference and practice book for intermediate students, Cambridge University Press.

Good general overview

Clancy, J. and Ballard, B. (1992), *How to Write Essays. A Practical Guide for Students,* Longman.

7
REPORT WRITING

by Sue Drew and Rosie Bingham

CONTENTS

This SkillPack aims to improve your report writing skills. The way you write a report for an assignment will have a significant influence on your grade.

What is the difference between a report and an essay? Essays are mainly used in education. They use information to explore ideas and arguments, and their main purpose is to practise these skills and demonstrate your abilities to lecturers.

"A report is a communication of information or advice from a person who has collected and studied the facts, to a person who has asked for the report because they need it for a specific purpose" (Stanton, 1990:243).

Reports are the most usual way of communicating the results of projects or investigations – for employers, charities, government, political organisations. They should be concise and have a specific structure, unlike essays which may be more discursive.

People who need reports are busy. A good report is one you don't need to reread to understand the point.

Courses ask you to produce reports to give you practice in presenting information in a way which will be relevant to employment.

We suggest you use this SkillPack:

- **in relation to a particular report you are writing**
- **before you begin any work**
- **while you are gathering your information and writing your report.**

When you have completed it, you should be able to:

1 identify the purpose of the report and the needs and characteristics of the audience
2 include accurate information appropriate to the purpose and audience
3 produce a report in a format appropriate to the subject area, purpose and audience, and present it legibly, with a clear layout
4 use images to support or clarify main points
5 use language which is appropriate for the subject area, purpose and audience and use grammar, punctuation and spelling which follow standard conventions.

You should be able to use the elements of the skill on your course, with guidance and support from tutors, lecturers and others.

NOTES

7.1 THE PURPOSE OF THE REPORT: GETTING STARTED

- **Who** is your report for? What are the readers' needs and characteristics? For example, if your topic is technical but your readers are not technical people, you need to explain things in non-technical language.

- **What** is it for – to inform, persuade, recommend? Will it lead to decisions, or policies? For example, a report to property developers wanting to decide on the use of a building should indicate the options, costs and profits.

If in doubt, ask your lecturer for clarification.

Reader characteristics	Purposes

Implications for the report

7.2 PLANNING YOUR TIME:
GETTING STARTED

To meet your deadline it helps to break down what you need to do into sub-tasks, and to estimate how long each will take. On average, drafting, editing and presenting the report will take as long as gathering the information – it is common to underestimate this. In identifying your sub-tasks, refer back to your purpose (Section 7.1).

Sub-task	Time needed/deadline

NOTES

You might find "Organising Yourself and Your Time" helpful (see Contents).

NOTES

7.3 GATHERING INFORMATION

This SkillPack focuses on writing the report rather than on gathering information for it. "Gathering and Using Information" (see Contents) will help you here. However, the following points are particularly important.

- **Identifying your purpose will help you see what information you need.**
- **The reader should be able to trace your information.** This means that you will need a good recording system which contains all the details necessary for when you actually produce the report.
- **If you refer to a publication you need to give its author and date (eg *Stanton, 1990*).** If you quote from a publication you also need the page number (eg *Stanton, 1990: 243*). You should list all publications referred to at the end of your report (see Section 7.8 for the standard format). If in doubt, ask library staff for advice.
- **You need to refer to evidence for any arguments, views or conclusions.** If you have collected the evidence yourself (eg from an experiment or a survey) you need to include how you gathered it, as well as what the evidence is. Again, this means having a good recording system.
- **Information must be accurate.**
- **You may need permission to use the material** – eg from an author, employer or other source of the information. Libraries can help you.
- **Information must be relevant.** What should you include or omit? The following checklist may help.

✔

Is the information	
relevant to your purpose?	
relevant to your readers?	
necessary as evidence/as part of an explanation?	
up to date?	
accurate?	

You should identify the key points which must be included in your report.

Key points

7.4 THE STRUCTURE OF THE REPORT

7.4.1 Format

Since there is no correct format for a report, it helps to ask your lecturers what they expect – eg there may be an accepted way of producing a lab report on your course.

General rules which are applicable in most situations are:

- **Tell them what you are going to tell them.**
- **Tell them.**
- **Tell them what you have told them.**

The following gives examples of possible formats. Example 1 may be more appropriate for formal, large reports (eg government reports) rather than for a short report to colleagues. Examples 2, 3 and 4 may be more usual in courses.

1	2	3
(The preliminaries)	*Title page*	*(A possible format for a lab report)*
Title page	*Aims/objectives*	*Aims*
Terms of reference	*Methodology (eg methods for gathering information)*	*Methods*
Contents	*Findings*	*Results*
List of tables/figures	*Conclusions*	*Conclusions*
Foreword	*Recommendations*	
Acknowledgements	*References/bibliography*	
Abstracts/synopsis	*Appendices*	**4**
(The main part)		
Introduction		*Title page*
Findings		*Summary*
Conclusions		*Table of contents*
(Supplementary)		*Body of report*
References/bibliography		*(introductions, findings, conclusions)*
Appendices		*Appendices*
Index		*Index*
(From Stanton, 1990)		*(From Peel, 1990)*

The following clarifies the terms given in the above examples. However, note that not all the following elements are needed in all reports – eg an index is only needed for long reports where readers need to locate items; not all reports have terms of reference; a list of abbreviations/terminology might help if the readers are unfamiliar with them, but not otherwise.

- **Terms of reference.** Specification by those commissioning a report of what they want. Indicates the scope of the report (eg if the report is to consider chemical pollution in Yorkshire rivers, it would be outside its terms of reference to consider air pollution, or pollution in Devon).

- **Acknowledgements.** Thanks to people or organisations who have helped.

- **Abstract/synopsis.** A short paragraph at the beginning of a report which says what is in it and allows readers to see if it is relevant to them.

- **Summary.** Gives the key points. It can be used at the start so that those readers with no time to read the report can grasp the main points, or at the end to draw things together. It should only contain information covered in the main part and it should be short.

- **Aims.** The overall purpose of the report (eg to investigate chemical pollution in Yorkshire rivers).

- **Objectives.** More specifically what you want to achieve (eg to identify the causes of chemical pollution, to identify solutions).

- **Foreword.** Sets the scene (eg why the report is needed, why it is important).

- **Introduction.** Outlines what the report is about. May include background to the report, aims, objectives.

- **Method.** How you gathered information, where from and how much (eg if you used a survey, who was surveyed, how did you decide on the target group, how many were surveyed, how were they surveyed – by interviews or questionnaire?)

- **Findings/results.** Statement of what you found out (eg results of an experiment or a survey or a project) with the interpretation and analysis.

- **Conclusions.** Draws together your findings.

- **Recommendations.** What you think should happen.

- **References/bibliography.** References are items referred to in the report. A bibliography is of additional material not specifically referred to, but which readers may want to follow up.

- **Appendices.** Detailed information which is important but which may distract from the flow of the report can be included.

- **Index.** Alphabetical list of topics covered, with page or section numbers where they can be found.

NOTES

7.4.2 Presentation

Good presentation can make a report clearer. Pay attention to the following elements:

- **Overall impact.** Typed or word-processed reports are preferable; at the very least use very neat writing. Because blocks of text are offputting, break it down into short paragraphs. You should also consider cost. Is it worth spending a lot of time and money on the presentation, or will something simple but clear be adequate?

- **Headings.** Headings should be clearly ranked. If you look at this chapter you will see there are three styles of headings – one for main sections, one for sub-sections, and one for further sub-sections.

- **Numbering.** Numbering your sections makes the report easier to follow. An increasingly common system is to number a main section (eg 1), then for sub-sections to place a dot after the main section number and begin to number again (eg 1.1). You can continue to a further level.

Sometimes it can help to number each paragraph. It is easier to refer the reader to "para 4.5.2" than to "about half way down page 6". The following example gives possible headings and section numbers for a report on public transport in Sheffield.

Appendices are often numbered using Roman numerals (eg Appendix (iii)).

Example

1 INTRODUCTION
    1.1   **Background**
    1.2   **Aims**
    1.3   **Objectives**

2 METHODS
    2.1   **The questionnaire**
    2.2   **The sample group**

3 FINDINGS
    3.1   **Response rate**
    3.2   **Findings**
    3.2.1   Who are the transport users
    3.2.2   Transport routes
    3.2.3   Users' opinions of transport provision

4 CONCLUSIONS

5 RECOMMENDATIONS
    5.1   **Public transport**
    5.2   **Private transport**

6 REFERENCES

7 APPENDICES
    (i)   **The questionnaire**
    (ii)   **Summary tables**

7.4.3 Content

The content of the report should be ordered logically to fit the purpose. Possibilities are by chronology (ie what happened first goes first), by themes or by following a line of argument – eg if you want to persuade it may be a idea to start with a punchy key point. Refer back to the purpose which you identified in Section 7.1.

Outline your content in the box below.

Order for the content

7.5 APPROPRIATE LANGUAGE

- The language should reflect the purpose of the report and the readers' needs. Will the readers understand it?

- It helps to be precise (eg *"The victims may have been hit with a blunt instrument"*, – were they or weren't they?). A thesaurus or Gowers' *The Complete Plain Words* (1986) (see Section 7.8) can help in selecting words to use.

- Punctuation and spelling should follow standard conventions to avoid misunderstanding. A good dictionary is essential and, if using a word processor, a spellchecker is invaluable.

- Reports need to be concise and should be free from unnecessary padding and repetition. Can you "tighten up" your writing?

  eg *"Salaries which are paid to teachers make up 65% of the school budget"*.
  "Teachers' salaries make up 65% of the school budget".

  eg *"The committee took into consideration the adoption of the proposal"*.
  "The committee considered adopting the proposal".

- Abbreviations should be written in full at first mention, with the abbreviation in brackets; after this the abbreviation alone can be used – eg "Personal and Professional Development (PPD)", and thereafter simply "PPD".

- You need to be consistent – eg you should use the same abbreviation throughout (eg always *PPD*, not sometimes *Ppd* or *PpD*). To avoid confusion, be consistent in your punctuation, underlining, capital letters and style of bullet points.

- Lists or key points should be consistent in style. You can begin a point either by a dash (–) or a bullet (•), but it is best to stick to one or the other throughout the report.

- Look at examples of reports for your subject. What sort of language do they use?

In what areas do you need to improve your writing?

Improvements needed in my writing

7.6 USE OF IMAGES/VISUALS

Images/visuals are best used to make something clearer, rather than for mere decoration. Use them when: something is difficult to describe in words; to aid comprehension; to reinforce a verbal message; to make it easy to pick out information; to help the reader see relationships.

For example:

- **to display statistics** – tables or graphs
- **for appearance** – photographs
- **to show how something works** – diagrams, flow charts or algorithms.

For example, in car driving ...

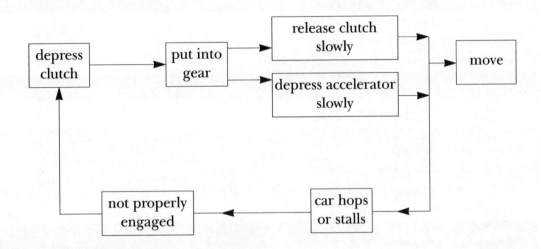

Some words of caution:

- **Will readers be familiar with your images?** For example, accountants may use "+" on a balance sheet for outgoings and "–" for income (for most of us the reverse seems more logical).
- **Are your visuals misleading?** A short book, referred to in Section 7.8, by Huff (1973), indicates how statistics can "lie".

Note down the images you wish to include below.

Images to be included

NOTES

7.7 EDITING

It can be useful to put your draft report aside for a few days before rereading it. In this way, you will be more distanced from it and be able to spot errors more easily. A word processor makes it easier to amend a report. The following checklist should help you edit your report.

7.7.1 Editing checklist

✔

The purpose	
Have you clarified your purpose?	
Have you identified your readers' needs/characteristics?	
Have you remembered these when considering the items below?	
Information	
Have you included the main points?	
Are points supported by evidence?	
Is the information relevant to the purpose?	
Accuracy	
Are there spelling mistakes?	
Is the grammar/punctuation correct?	
Do the figures add up?	
Are the references correct, in the text and at the end?	
Are all sources of information listed in the "References" section? Are abbreviations consistent?	
Images	
Are images clear?	
Format	
Is there a balance between sections?	
Do the most important items have the most space?	
Is the report easy to follow?	
Is it easy to find information in the report?	
Are headings and numbering clear?	
Are the arguments followed through? Is it logical/easy to follow?	
Language	
Is it clear, direct, easy to read?	
Will the readers understand it?	
Will its tone help you achieve the purpose?	
Can unnecessary words/phrases be deleted?	
Is there any repetition?	
Presentation	
Is the layout appealing?	
Does it highlight important points?	

Finally, it's a good idea to keep a copy of your report and background notes, just in case the reader loses it, you need to revise it, you need to produce a further report or somebody wants to check your data.

7.8 REFERENCES AND BIBLIOGRAPHY

Libraries may have materials on this skill. The following give examples:

Bell, J. (1987), *Doing your Research Project: A Guide for First-time Researchers in Education and Social Science,* Open University Press.

Cooper, B. M. (1964), *Writing Technical Reports,* Penguin Books.

Gowers, E. (1986), *The Complete Plain Words,* HMSO.

Huff, D. (1973), *How to Lie with Statistics,* Penguin Books.

Peel, M. (1990), *Improving Your Communication Skills,* Kogan Page.

Stanton, N. (1990), *Communication,* Macmillan Education.

8 ORAL PRESENTATION

by Sue Drew and Rosie Bingham

CONTENTS

On many courses students are required to give seminar papers, or make individual or group presentations about their work. This is because employers want to recruit graduates or higher diplomates with good verbal skills, and giving presentations as part of courses helps students practise these skills. Some jobs require you to make oral presentations and others may not but they do require the same verbal communication skills used for making presentations – presenting information, arguing a case, persuading, negotiating, explaining.

Some students have better verbal than written skills. Presentations provide an alternative way for students to demonstrate their abilities.

This SkillPack aims to help you make better presentations and to combat the nervousness which most of us experience.

We suggest you use this SkillPack:

- **to help you prepare for a particular individual or group presentation.**

When you have completed it, you should be able to:

1 select material which is appropriate for the purpose and the audience
2 structure material for the purpose and the audience
3 prepare relevant visual aids which clearly illustrate points (eg legible OHP slides)
4 present visual aids effectively and at appropriate junctures
5 use language, tone and manner (including non-verbal behaviour) suited to the purpose and audience
6 listen to and effectively answer questions
7 for group presentations, allocate tasks so that each member has a role.

You should be able to use the above elements of the skill in your course, with guidance and support from your tutors and others.

8.1 INTRODUCTION

You might find it helpful to compare a presentation you enjoyed with one you found boring and uninteresting. What were the main differences?

The following is similar to the assessment sheets used by tutors to judge presentations. You can use it to help you identify what you feel you can do very well and areas to which you need to give attention. It uses a scale where 1 = "very well" and 4 = "needs considerable attention".

✔

Aims for the presentation	1	2	3	4
being clear about them yourself				
making them clear to the audience				

Material	1	2	3	4
researching				
arguing/explaining it				
making it relevant to the topic/audience				

The delivery	1	2	3	4
keeping to time				
having a varied mix of inputs/visual aids				
having relevant visual aids				
having clear visual aids				
making it appropriate for the topic/audience/aims				
getting audience involvement/interest				
being confident				
projecting voice/self/content				
dealing with questions				

This SkillPack deals with all the above issues.

8.2 THE CONTEXT

8.2.1 Aims

Is the presentation to inform, train, persuade, entertain, sell or demonstrate? Being clear about its purpose helps you decide what to include or omit, and what approach to use. For example:

- if the presentation is to **inform** or **explain** it helps to have a logical order and to use examples and analogies (eg *"It's a bit like ..."*)

- if the presentation is to **persuade** it helps to be convincing, use evidence and show enthusiasm.

Another useful technique is to ask yourself increasingly focused questions. For example:

- What is the **subject** (eg *"access for the disabled to buildings"*)?

- What is the **theme** (eg *"how to improve this access"*)?

- What is the **point** or **"angle"**? (eg *"current access is really inadequate"*)?

- What are the **objectives**/what do you want to achieve (eg *"to encourage better access"*)?

Aims	Theme	Point/angle	Objectives

8.2.2 The audience

- **Who will your audience be?**
- **What will they expect or need?**
- **How many will there be? One lecturer, other students, a mix?**
- **What will their interests and level of knowledge be?**

To pitch a presentation correctly you must consider the audience in terms of their level of knowledge, the degree of formality and the type of language used.

Audience characteristics	Implications for presentation

NOTES

8.2.3 Time

How long will your presentation be? The time may be specified by the tutor, but if you can decide for yourself you will find that 20 minutes is probably the maximum time. More than that can be tedious for the audience. If you have longer than 20 minutes to fill, you could try to break your presentation up with different types of activity (see later sections for suggestions). Allow time at the beginning for people to settle. Will you allow time for questions? If it is a group presentation how will you divide the time between the presenters?

8.2.4 The room

The location and seating arrangement can influence what you do. It helps to look at the room in advance.

Presenter	Presenter	Presenter
Enables discussion, but many will find it difficult to see the visual aids.	Enables discussion, but some will find it difficult to see the visual aids.	Best layout for a talk. Limits discussion. Audience can see visual aids well.

8.3 PREPARING MATERIAL

NOTES

Preparing your material in good time will reduce anxiety and knowing your topic well increases confidence. If preparing for a group presentation you need to come to a clear agreement on who is preparing what material. Putting it in writing can avoid confusion.

8.3.1 Selecting material

"Gathering and Using Information" (see Contents) will help you assemble your information. You should then consider how to select your material bearing in mind your aims, audience, the time allowed and the room. The following questions may help:

- **Is all your material relevant to your aims and audience?**

- **What key messages do you want to put across?**

- **How long will it take to deliver the material?** (A rehearsal, possibly in front of a friend, may help you find out)

- **What could you omit if you run out of time?**

- **What are the absolute essentials?** (Audiences tend to be able to take in less than you think)

- **What could be added if you have time to spare?**

8.3.2 Structuring the material

How could the material be ordered? You could write it up, get an overview and decide on an order, or write the main points on cards and shuffle them until the best order emerges.

General rules are as follows:
- **Tell them what you are going to tell them (the beginning).**
- **Tell them (the middle).**
- **Tell them what you have told them (the end).**

Tell them what you are going to tell them (the beginning)

Making the format clear to the audience at the start tells them what to expect (eg *"Please could you leave questions until the end"; "Please ask questions as we go through"*).

Outline the content you will cover (eg *"I am going to talk about the poor provision for disabled people"*).

You need to set the tone and grab attention. Do something you feel comfortable with. Beginnings can include:

- a question
- a true story
- a provocative statement
- a quotation
- a visual aid
- a joke (but take care – if it is not funny, it can embarrass)
- a surprise (eg a surprising statistic).

Tell them (the middle)

Ordering the material into "chunks" rather than flitting from one point to another helps the audience to follow your words. You need to decide on the best order for your "chunks" (eg for the topic of disability: you could "chunk" by type of disability or by problems faced). The following questions may help:

- Are you explaining something where one step follows from another?
- Is date or time order important?
- Do you need to give one side of an argument, then the next?

Without structure audiences can become confused or bored.

The following are ways of creating structure:

- **verbal clues** (eg *"We've looked at the access problems for disabled people; now we'll look at possible solutions"*)
- **visual aids** (eg a new OHP transparency can signal a change of topic or new point)
- **varied activities** (eg asking for questions, asking if the audience have understood before moving on)
- for group presentations, using **different presenters** (eg *"Now Jane will look at ..."*).

Tell them what you have told them (the end)

Possible ways of ending the presentation include the following:

- Briefly repeat the main points and draw them together.
- Emphasise the main point or "angle" (some of the "beginnings" can be useful here too – a visual aid or an anecdote).
- If discussion was involved, review the main points or future implications (eg *"It looks like we need to focus on ...in the future"*)
- Thank the audience.

8.3.3 Speaker's notes

Speaker's notes are important, especially if you are nervous, but listening to a speaker reading a script can be boring and uninteresting for the audience. There are various ways of making notes, and you can choose the one which works for you:

- **Cards.** Put each main point with notes on a card and number the cards.
- **OHP slides.** Use them to remind you of the points.
- **Notes under bold headings on sheets of paper.** Margins can be used to indicate how long each section should take (and, in group presentations, who is covering it).
- **Fully written-out text.** Use this method for difficult sections, but rehearse, and use the notes to reassure, not to read from.
- **Mind maps.** For example:

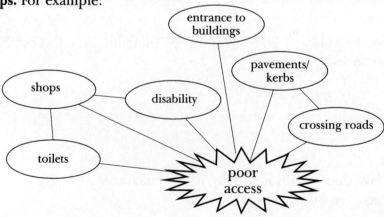

8.4 PREPARING AND USING VISUAL AIDS

8.4.1 Preparation

> **Visual aids grab attention, help the audience understand, make the presentation look professional, and help you if you are nervous (the audience will look at the visual aid – not at you).**

They should be clear, usable, visible, so make them big and bold, avoid pastel colours and keep words to a minimum if using an OHP. What would have more impact as an OHP slide – using the above paragraph or the format below?

> **Visual aids**
>
> - **get attention**
> - **aid understanding**
> - **look professional**
> - **help nerves**

8.4.2 Usage

Keeping them simple is good, and making them complex can cause problems. An audience cannot focus on too many things at once, so try not to use too many visual aids (think of watching friends' holiday slides!).

It is also important to make good use of the visual aids you decide to use as the audience will be confused if you don't refer to them – practise using them in advance. When using visual aids look at the audience, not at the aids.

Different visual aids suit different purposes (see below).

Cheap/simple ↑ ↓ *More complex/expensive*

Visual aid	Good for...	Cautions
Black/white-board	Spontaneous use, simple messages, permanent background information.	Have spare pen, chalk, duster, rubber. Use quickly, can interrupt flow.
Flipchart	Background information, revealing successive bits of "story", can record ideas from discussions and be kept for future reference.	Cumbersome to use. Needs to be bold. Leaving it up can distract.
Overhead projector (OHP)	Prepared slides, or acetate slides which can be written on during presentation. Can have complex "overlays" of slides.	Turn off when not using. Cover words not referring to as can distract. Get slides in right order (paper between each one helps). Check the slides are the right way up and that all the slide appears on the screen. Learn to focus in advance.
Slide projector	Real photos. Makes an impact.	Use preloaded magazine. Check slides are right way up. Learn to focus in advance. Can leave slides on too long/short a time. Can inhibit discussion.
Video	Real/live input. Entertaining.	Load, rewind, check sound/picture in advance. Select sections to use.
Film	Real/live input. Entertaining.	Have a projectionist. Preview the material. Have a contingency plan in case the film breaks.
Objects (models experiments, products)	Demonstrations. Makes an impact. Explains a process. Makes a dry subject interesting.	Model/experiment – ensure it will work. Big enough to see. Allow time to pass item round the audience. Can distract.

8.5 THE DELIVERY

8.5.1 Organisation

Being well organised helps. Try, within the room's limits, to organise seating in advance or just before the presentation starts. Arriving at the last minute means you can be thrown off balance if all is not as expected (eg the OHP is not working or the seating is in the wrong arrangement).

Have your notes and visual aids handy and ordered – being unable to find something can fluster you.

8.5.2 Timekeeping

Put your watch where you can see it easily or, for group presentations, give each other warnings (eg *"You've got two minutes left"*). Running over time leaves other speakers less time, can ruin the organisation of the event and can bore the audience.

A rehearsal can help.

8.5.3 Voice and manner

If you suspect that your voice is monotonous break your speech up: use visual aids; ask questions of the audience; change pace; use pauses.

Your mannerisms may be distracting – eg swaying, playing with your hair, covering your mouth, fidgeting. You can identify any irritating mannerisms by asking others for feedback or videoing your presentation. Then decide what you do about them (eg give your hands something to do, such as holding prompt cards).

In group presentations the behaviour of those not currently speaking can distract – eg chatting, passing notes, looking uninterested.

Good visual aids help, but practise using them. Turning your back on the audience or looking at the OHP screen may prevent them from hearing you, and break "rapport". Use a pointer (such as a pen).

It is essential to relate to your audience – eg by making eye contact (try not to stare at one individual but to 'scan' the group). Can the audience see and hear you? If you are not sure, ask them. If you speak quietly, practise projecting your voice. Speak to the person at the back of the room, not the front.

Delivery techniques that would particularly help me

8.5.4 Dealing with questions

This should not be difficult if you are well prepared.

- **Check that you understand the question.**

- **Admit ignorance rather than waffle.**

- **If you are unsure of the answer, you could pass the question back to the questioner** (eg *"What do you think?"*). This can generate discussion.

- **In a group presentation select somebody to chair the questions session so that questioners address that person, s/he checks what the question means and then asks somebody in the group to reply.** The "chair" will also decide how many questions to take, and when to end the session (eg *"Thank you. We need to move on/end now"*).

8.6 COMBATING NERVES

Being prepared and organised can be **the** biggest help in combating nerves, as can:

- **rehearsing in advance**

- **reminding yourself that everybody feels nervous.** Audiences often don't notice nerves and, if they do, will make allowances

- **asking what is the worst thing that could happen and preparing for it** (eg Drying up – have good speaker's notes to prevent drying up – awkward questions – prepare answers in advance to any potentially awkward questions)

- **trying to relax.** Relaxation techniques include deep breathing, tensing and then relaxing muscles, visualising a pleasant scene. Leaving everything to the last minute will increase tension

- **having a glass of water at hand.**

What do you usually do when you are nervous? What could you do about it? Who or what might help? You may find "Coping with Pressure" (see Contents) helpful.

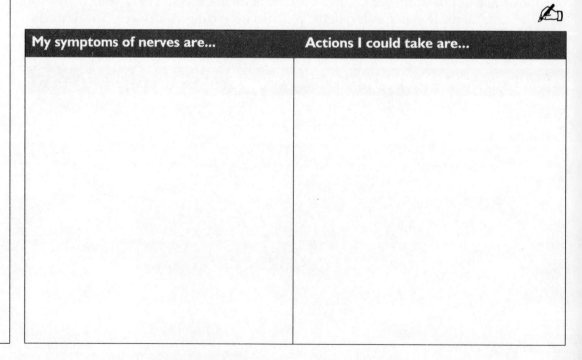

My symptoms of nerves are...	Actions I could take are...

8.7 PRESENTATION CHECKLIST

Are you prepared? The following checklist can act as a reminder:

Identify aims.	
Identify audience characteristics.	
Identify time allowance for the presentation.	
Check out the room.	
Get material together.	
Decide on a format and structure.	
For group presentations, divide up roles and tasks for preparation and on the day.	
Make speaker's notes.	
Prepare visual aids.	
Prepare the delivery: • the beginning • the middle • the end.	
Prepare for the question session.	
Cope with nerves.	
Be organised on the day.	

Watching others' presentations (there may be videos available in some libraries) and getting feedback on your presentations can be very helpful.

NOTES

8.8 REFERENCES AND BIBLIOGRAPHY

Libraries may have materials on this skill area. The following give examples:

Bernstein, D. (1988), *Put It Together. Put It Across. The Craft of Business Presentation*, Cassell.

Peel, M. (1990), *Improving your Communication Skills*, Kogan Page.

Stanton, N. (1990), *Communication*, Macmillan Education.

Videos

The Floor is Yours Now – A Guide to Successful Presentations Gower, (24 minutes).

We Can't Hear You at The Back (part of a series – *Work is a Four-letter Word*) BBC, 1992 (30 minutes).

Laser Disks

Discovering Presentations, (interactive video) – Longmans Training: British Telecom 1991.

9
SOLVING PROBLEMS

by Sue Drew and Rosie Bingham

CONTENTS

Being able to solve problems is very important in all professional areas. How can systems or processes operate more effectively? How can difficulties between people be resolved? How can transport, medical or engineering problems be solved?

This SkillPack aims to help you solve the problems likely to be encountered on your course. Courses include assignments or activities designed to help students develop the ability to solve problems – eg case studies, projects, experiments. Improving your skills in this area will help you get better grades or marks.

We suggest you use this SkillPack:

- **in relation to a particular assignment or activity which involves solving a problem**
- **before you start work on that assignment or activity**
- **whilst you are working on it.**

When you have completed it, you should be able to:

1. collect sufficient information to clarify critical features of the problem and identify possible solutions
2. select relevant information
3. identify critical features of problems which include a broad range of factors and a range of possible solutions
4. where appropriate, accurately follow set procedures to clarify the problem, seek information and identify solutions
5. identify and select efficient and effective procedures to clarify the problem, seek information and identify solutions
6. identify and use criteria to select an effective solution (eg short-term and long-term benefits).

You should be able to use the above elements of this skill on your course and in your personal life, with guidance and support from tutors, lecturers and others.

9.1 WHAT DO YOU CURRENTLY DO?

Here are three problems. Spend 5-10 minutes solving one or more of them as far as possible within the time. Use the checklist below to note what you are doing. This will help you discover how you tend to solve problems. Doing the exercise in pairs, with one person problem solving and the other recording the process, could be useful.

Problem 1 You keep seven pairs of socks unsorted in a drawer. If you just pull out a pair at random they never seem to match. What is the minimum number of socks you would have to pull out to be sure that you get a matching pair?

Problem 2 How long will it take to complete an assignment you currently have to do?

Problem 3 Your notes are so disorganised that you can't find those you need. What system would help you find notes more easily?

✔

Calculating	
Mentally picturing	
Sketching	
Writing a list	
Thinking about something else entirely	
Feeling anxious	
Any other activities (list):	

Which methods did you use to solve the above problems? Which others are you familiar with?

✔

	In this exercise	Familiar with
The logical approach – definite steps which you go through		
Trial and error – try ideas until one works		
Creative idea generation – think of lots of ideas		
Rational choice from alternatives – weighing up the advantages and disadvantages		
Other methods (please specify):		

It may help to ask others how they normally solve problems. There can be a tendency to think our way is the only way.

There are a range of different ways to solve problems. The method chosen depends to some extent on the type of problem; problem 1 above had a right answer, whereas the other two did not. However, each of us has **preferred** approaches.

9.2 POSSIBLE PROBLEM-SOLVING TECHNIQUES

The following briefly describes a variety of approaches. You could adapt them to the problem you are currently facing.

9.2.1 A design process

This approach is often used to design manufactured products and organisational systems.

1 **Needs evaluation.** (What is the purpose of the object or system?).
   - What are the user's needs?
   - What are the circumstances in which it will be used?
   - What might be the benefits of having or using it?

2 **Design specification.** (What are the requirements of the design?).
   - Cost factors
   - Evaluation of other products
   - Safety standards
   - Quantities required
   - Manufacturing facilities available.

3 **Concept or solution generation.** This is the creative part of the process – generating a wide range of possible solutions.

4 **Solution evaluation.** This involves detailed consideration of how well each solution or concept satisfies the needs identified and the design specifications.

5 **Detailed design.** This takes the selected solution and ensures that it will work.

6 **Review.** This ensures that the final product satisfies the criteria in 1 and 2 above before moving on to implementation.

9.2.2 The GRASP® (Getting Results and Solving Problems) approach

This is recommended by the Comino Foundation (1994).

Stage 1
Select the purpose or objectives and the criteria for success.

- Have you pictured the situation you would like to bring about?
- Are you clear what you are trying to achieve and why, as opposed to what you would like to do?
- How will you know when you have succeeded?
- Are you committed to act and succeed?

Stage 2
Generate different ways of achieving the objective and select the best.

- Have you identified as many ways of achieving the objectives as possible?
- What constraints must be observed in any action you take?

Stage 3
Put the chosen plan into operation and control the process.

- How will you control the course of events and stay on the right path?

Stage 4
Review continually each operation and the results.

- Is the original purpose still valid?
- Is the original course of action still valid?
- Are the criteria too loose or rigid?
- Are you receiving sufficient feedback and are you acting on it?

9.2.3 Following set procedures

For some areas, particularly where safety is involved, you need to follow set procedures accurately. This may apply to laboratory work, for example.

In this case you should to clarify anything you don't understand with your lecturer or tutor. If you fail to find a solution you may have to backtrack to see if you have followed the procedures correctly.

9.2.4 Trial and error

If you find it difficult to get started or you become anxious when confronted with a problem, it can help to first try something – anything – to remove the block. Possibilities are:

- **Do it now.** Scribble down ideas immediately then return to them later go back and review them.

- **"Quantity not quality"**. Get plenty of scrap paper and write as many ideas and thoughts about the problem as possible.

In certain situations trial and error may be dangerous – eg when electrical experiments won't work. Using trial and error can also take up more time than thinking things through in advance.

GRASP® is the registered trademark of the Comino Foundation

NOTES

9.2.5 Creative idea generation

Brainstorming

This works best with a group but you can do it alone. If you are in a group, get one person to write down whatever is said on a board or flip-chart where all can see it. It can be helpful to set a time limit – eg 10 minutes. Use the following steps:

- **Write down any ideas however unusual, impractical or rude** (don't judge or select at this stage).
- **Encourage "piggy backing"** (adding ideas to other people's ideas, even if at this stage they seem to be far off the point).
- **Do not make judgements about the ideas.** Your concern is to generate ideas creatively at this stage.

When you have finished generating ideas:

- **If in a group, start to check what people meant.**
- **Whether in a group or alone, group similar ideas together.**
- **Judge which ones look suitable and which ones don't.**

Left brain/right brain

According to some theories, the two sides of our brains have different ways of handling information.

LEFT BRAIN	RIGHT BRAIN
Connects with the right hand.	Connects with the left hand.
Analyses, abstracts, counts, marks time, plans step-by-step procedures, verbalises, makes logical, rational statements.	Understands metaphors, dreams, creates new combinations of ideas, makes gestures to communicate.

The aim in **creative** problem solving is to encourage the right brain process. Try the following:

- **Work at the best time and in the best place for creative thinking.** You will have to work this out from experience. Some of us work best after midnight, others at 6 am in the morning, some while listening to music, others in silence.
- **Use a different communication process** – eg if you have been talking about a problem, stop talking and draw, mime, generate computer images.
- **Don't think about it** – eg go to sleep or for a walk, since ideas often emerge when you least expect them.
- **"Reframe" the problem or look at it from another angle** – eg look at a problem object upside down or see the spaces or voids in an object rather than the solid parts.
- **Use unrelated objects to "unblock" yourself** – eg after brainstorming a problem for a while, add one or two completely unrelated objects and consider how these objects could be used to solve the problem.

9.2.6 Constructive analysis

Having generated ideas, how do you choose between them? According to Edward de Bono (1982) we tend to make decisions about problems in an emotional, rather than rational, way.

De Bono's method is to think of solutions to a problem and then write down in three columns the **plus**, **minus** and **interesting** aspects of each solution.

By "interesting" he means any consequences of the decision that are neither negative nor positive. The plus and minus columns can focus on facts and the "interesting" column allows the mind to wander over consequences.

9.3 SOLVING YOUR PROBLEM

With the exception of those areas which require you to follow a set procedure, there is normally no single best way to solve a problem. It may therefore be helpful to try out an approach which is different from the ones you normally use. You can then see if it works better, if you prefer your usual approach, or if you could merge the approaches in some way.

Using an approach which is totally alien can inhibit your creativity – but so can failing to try new ones.

Whichever of the approaches suggested in Section 9.2 you try it will help to ask yourself the following questions.

Have you identified the essential elements of the problem?
eg Why is it a problem? For whom? What is problematic?

NOTES

NOTES

Have you got enough information about the problem to help you begin to solve it?
eg Context – what factors do you need to bear in mind about the situation surrounding the problem? What are the constraints, ie what might limit any solutions? Cost? Time? Physical limits of space or size?

What are the possible advantages or benefits to do with the problem?

NOTES

Have you generated a range of possible solutions? (At this stage it helps to identify as many as possible)

How can you select the best solution? *eg What criteria can you judge it by? How will you know if it is a good solution?*

NOTES

Have you had to follow set procedures to solve your problem? Have you yourself worked out how to solve it?
eg What procedures did you use? Did they work? Did you follow them accurately?

Procedure	Effectiveness

Have you selected a solution? If not what else do you need to do to help you select one?

NOTES

Have you tried out the approaches suggested in Section 2?

Which approach(es) did you use?

What was useful and why?

What was not useful and why?

NOTES

9.4 REFERENCES AND BIBLIOGRAPHY

Libraries may have materials on this skill area. The following give examples:

Comino Foundation (1994), *GRASP® – Getting Results and Solving Problems*, Comino Foundation, 29 Holloway Lane, Amersham, HP6 6DJ

Cowan, J. (nd), *Individual Approaches to Problem Solving*, Department of Civil Engineering, Heriot Watt University.

de Bono, E. (1982), *De Bono's Thinking Course*, Ariel Books, BBC.

10
GROUP WORK
by Sue Drew and Rosie Bingham

CONTENTS

Group work can cover any activity involving working with others – eg group projects, lab work, seminars, tutorials. Group work means being able to share resources, ideas and abilities. You may find that your course assesses your skills in this area.

Courses include group work because employers see evidence of group work skills as very important when recruiting graduates or higher diplomates. All jobs involve working with others.

Group effectiveness depends not on luck and the composition of the group, but rather on individual members' skills in dealing with each other. These skills can be improved by practice, and students can learn from and help each other.

The other key element to success is to not only focus on end results but also on how to get there.

We suggest you use this SkillPack:

- **right at the start of any group work**
- **as you continue, to help improve your work and avoid problems.**

When you have completed it, you should be able to:

1 clarify and understand group goals
2 plan actions to meet goals and review group and individual progress
3 agree allocation of tasks
4 carry them out within agreed limits
5 contribute to meetings in a way which is relevant and equal
6 listen actively to others
7 request feedback on individual performance (relating to tasks and behaviour)
8 identify elements of personal behaviour which are effective or less effective in a group situation

You should be able to use the above elements of this skill on your course or programme, with guidance and support from tutors, lecturers and other students on your course.

10.1 INTRODUCTION

In what sort of groups have you operated up until now? Sporting? Social? Family? Work? Identifying what you have liked or disliked about them may give you clues about areas you will enjoy or find difficult in your course group work.

Type of group	Positives	Difficulties

10.2 CONTRIBUTING TO GROUPS

10.2.1 Ground rules

It is very helpful to establish a set of rules ("ground rules") to guide the way in which your group will operate. Following ground rules will make meetings run smoothly, prevent problems and give you some control if group members are difficult. You could use the following set of rules as it stands or agree, as a group, to add or delete items. You can then use the rules as you work. Either put them on the wall or take it in turns to monitor them, for example, by appointing a timekeeper for meetings.

Suggested ground rules
Always attend meetings.
Agree an agenda for meetings.
Nobody to speak for longer than three minutes at a time.
No interrupting.
No putting others down. Criticise the ideas not the person.
Encourage everyone to speak.
Start and end meetings on time.
Set deadlines and stick to them.
Everyone to do what they agree.

Add any further items identified by your group

10.2.2 Your behaviour

Does your behaviour as an individual contribute to the group's effectiveness? Score yourself on the chart below using the following scale, at the start of your group work, in the middle and at the end. It has a scale of 1-4 where 1 = "very positive" and 4 is "very negative".

✔

Positive behaviour	1	2	3	4	Negative behaviour
Listening to others, asking for clarification (eg *"did you mean ...?"*)					Interrupting, putting others down
Expressing relevant views positively					Being negative, disrupting, being irrelevant
Contributing equally					Keeping quiet, dominating
Asking what others think about your contributions					Unconcerned about others' views
Pulling your weight, doing an equal part of the work					Letting others do the work, not turning up
Meeting deadlines					Missing deadlines

10.3 GROUP GOALS

Being clear about group goals is an essential first step. You can prevent later problems caused by misunderstandings by asking each member what they think the group is supposed to be doing and achieving. You may need to ask your tutor to clarify what is expected.

What do you want to achieve as a group? (eg related to the task or how you work together)	What do you want to achieve as individuals? (eg learning something, a good grade)

10.4 PLANNING ACTIONS AND ALLOCATING TASKS

Planning how to meet your goals can avoid wasted effort and problems, and make the most of your resources. Answering the following questions may help:

- **How can the task be subdivided into smaller tasks?**
- **When must each sub-task be completed?**
- **Who can do which sub-tasks?**
- **What will you do about the sub-tasks nobody wants to do (eg negotiate, draw straws)?**
- **Does the workload seem equally distributed?**
- **If you carry out all the sub-tasks by the time agreed, will all your goals be met?**

You may find three Starter SkillPacks useful in planning your work: "Organising Yourself and Your Time", "Negotiating and Assertiveness", and "Solving Problems" (see Contents).

Task	To be done by (group member)	Deadline

How will the group check everybody has completed their agreed tasks? More importantly, how will you ensure that you do what you have agreed?

10.5 DEALING WITH PROBLEMS

Identifying the cause of a problem can often help the group to solve it. The following are examples of typical problems and suggested ways of dealing with them; but they are suggestions only and you may have other ideas.

Problem	Possible solution
Uneven workload, "passengers", people not pulling their weight	Agree who does what at the start, and write it down to avoid confusion. Ask those not pulling their weight why not – they may have a good reason. Explain to them the effect it is having on the group. Consider using the SkillPack on "Negotiating and Assertiveness" (see Contents).
Too much work involved	Reread the project brief – have you misunderstood? Are there more efficient ways of carrying out the task? Consider using the SkillPack on "Organising Yourself and Your Time" (see Contents).
Confusion	Discuss your goals as a group and keep referring back to them. Consider using the SkillPack on "Solving Problems" (see Contents).
Quiet group members	Ask for their views; encourage them to speak; be positive about their comments.
Disruptive group members eg clowning around, negativeness, over-talkativeness, aggression	Possibilities include: ignoring jokes; asking "talkatives" to let somebody else have a say; pointing out when somebody is negative and asking for positives. Consider using the SkillPack on "Negotiating and Assertiveness" (see Contents).

If you or your group encounters a problem which you are unable to deal with, you may need to seek further help from your tutor.

10.6 IDENTIFYING YOUR OWN GROUP SKILLS

This section focuses not on other people's behaviour but on how **you** work with other people. Your behaviour will influence their behaviour and you have a better chance of changing what **you** do.

The following will help you to clarify your behaviour in groups. You might like to ask those you have worked with or your tutors:

- **what they thought about how you did the work**
- **what they thought about how you behaved in the group.**

Aspects I enjoy; things I'm good at in groups	Aspects I find difficult; things I need to improve in groups

NOTES

NOTES

10.7 REFERENCES AND BIBLIOGRAPHY

Libraries may have materials on this skill. The following give examples:

Johnson, D. W. and Johnson, F. P. (1991), *Joining Together: Group Theory and Group Skills*, Prentice Hall.

11
NEGOTIATING AND ASSERTIVENESS

by Sue Drew and Rosie Bingham

CONTENTS

Negotiating is the process of coming to an agreement with others. **Assertiveness** is about getting what you want, whilst respecting the needs of others.

We continually find ourselves in situations where we need to negotiate or be assertive (eg which film should we go to see? Who will do the washing up?). Situations in which you might need to negotiate or be assertive are: in group work, ensuring all contribute fairly; in setting up placements or agreeing projects. This will help you to get the most out of a course and obtain good grades or marks.

In employment these skills are often crucial, as virtually all jobs involve making agreements with colleagues. In many jobs negotiating is a principal aspect – eg managing others; buying; selling; legal work; surveying; project management and so on.

We suggest you use this SkillPack:

- **when you face a situation where you need to negotiate or be assertive.**

When you have completed it, you should be able to:

1 identify, by seeking feedback from others, your own reactions and usual responses to pressure
2 identify sources of pressure
3 evaluate the effectiveness of your own reactions and responses, and identify needs for change
4 plan short-term goals related to needs for change, and plan necessary actions
5 identify and use sources of support
6 put plans into action, record and review progress.

You should be able to use the above elements of the skill both on your course and in your personal life with guidance and support from tutors, lecturers and others.

11.1 NEGOTIATING SKILLS

11.1.1 Your approach

There are various approaches to negotiating. These include:

- **coercion** (eg *"If you don't agree then..."*)
- **use of emotion** (eg *"I've struggled here on this broken leg, the least you could do is..."*)
- **"brinkmanship"** (eg *"I'll resign unless..."*)
- **"divide and rule"** (eg *"...but...Fred didn't say that..."*)
- **"deliberate misunderstanding"** (eg *"It's 40p for one"*, *"40p for one hundred is quite reasonable"*)
  (Steel, Murphy and Russill, 1989).

This SkillPack makes the central assumption that using force or "tricks" is counterproductive.

Firstly, we may have to work again with those with whom we negotiate. Secondly, the organisation we represent may need to maintain goodwill or a reputation for ethical conduct.

How do you normally try to get what you want? Does it work? What effect does it have on others?

Techniques I use	Effects

For what reasons do you think you sometimes fail to agree things, whether with friends, family, or colleagues?

	Often	Some-times	Never
I dislike the other people.			
I'm afraid of the other people.			
I find people difficult.			
I try to please others too much.			
I get sidetracked.			
I have misunderstandings with others.			
I fall into conflicts with others.			
I do not know what I want.			
I have few ideas for solutions.			
I make poor decisions.			
I dislike losing face.			
Others (please add your own):			

11.1.2 An approach to negotiating

One approach is proposed below. After each set of suggestions (based on a book by Fisher and Ury (1987)) a box is provided for your comments about how you could use them in a situation which is confronting you. Throughout this section we use the following scenario as an example:

Five students are working on a group project. "A" has not produced a graph for the group report as promised.

Separate the people from the problem

- Identify problems and issues rather than focusing on personalities (eg not *"They are just awkward"* but *"Why don't they like the idea?"*)
- Consider the people. It's easy to see them as "the other side", not as individuals. What is their perspective on the problem? You don't have to agree with their view, but acknowledging it can help. What are their feelings? Involving them can encourage commitment (eg not *"This is what we've agreed; what do you think?"* but *"How should we go about it?"*)

Example

- ***Problem:*** *What work still has to be done for the group project? When is the deadline? What are the difficulties?*
- ***People:*** *How do we, and "A", feel about it (worried, guilty, angry, not bothered)?*

How I could use this suggestion

Focus on interests not positions

If you take up a firm position it can be hard to shift from it without losing face (eg *"If you don't support me, I'll resign"*). An alternative approach is to explore interests. This might reveal common concerns as well as differences (eg to find a solution to a problem so you can work together).

You could ask all parties to list their interests and see where they coincide. You could find out the interests of others by questioning "Why?" or "Why not?".

Example

What matters most to the members of the group? A good grade? Sharing work equally? Maintaining friendships?

This may influence the option you choose.

How I could use this suggestion

NOTES

NOTES

Generate options before making decisions

Having a number of options can lead to better decisions. Obstacles to generating options include having a "bottom line" which limits your thinking, although you may actually need a bottom line so that you all work to the same end (eg the group project deadline). Other obstacles include looking for a single answer, assuming a fixed situation, seeing the problem as belonging to someone else, or making judgements too early. It can be better to have several options, to separate options from decisions, and to generate ideas first without evaluating them.

It helps to know what you'll do if you don't reach agreement (the better the alternative, the greater your power – eg *"I don't really need to sell the house, I could rent it out"*) and to work out what are other possible alternatives.

Example

The options for dealing with the group work project problem may depend on the interests of the group members and the reasons why "A" is not doing the work. Options may include: "A" does it; the others do it and it is submitted as from all five members, or it is submitted as the work of four people minus "A"; the report is submitted without "A"'s graph; the matter is referred to a tutor.

How I could use this suggestion

Agree criteria against which to judge solutions

Agreeing the principles by which you operate, and the criteria for judging whether the solution was successful, can prevent face-saving problems (eg not *"Did you win or lose?"*, but *"Was the end result of our project good?"*).

Establishing criteria in advance can forestall problems (eg by making equal contributions to the project into a criterion by which to judge success and getting everybody to agree to this means that you have some comeback if one person fails to contribute).

Example

What matters most in this group project? A good grade or mark? Sharing work equally? Maintaining friendships? This may influence the option chosen.

How I could use this suggestion

Yes...but

What if there is a row, or "A" won't talk to us about the group project, or we daren't broach the subject? Do we just put up with it? This is where assertiveness comes in.

NOTES

11.2 ASSERTIVENESS SKILLS

11.2.1 What is assertiveness?

Our behaviour towards others can be described as falling into the following categories. These are not fixed, as we may behave differently in different situations with different people.

* **Passive.** Allowing others to get what they want, not expressing your needs (eg *"You have the chocolate cake"*).
* **Aggressive.** Imposing your will or needs on others (eg *"Give me that chocolate cake"*).
* **Manipulative.** "Scheming" to get what you want (eg *"No, no, you have the chocolate cake, I'll go without"*).
* **Assertive.** Expressing your needs openly without imposing on the other (eg *"I like chocolate cake, do you? Should we divide it up?"*).

How do you tend to use any of the above behaviours, in which situations – perhaps on your course – and with which people?

Situation	People	Behaviour

Your behaviour can affect other people in the following ways:

- Being **passive** can make others feel powerful or frustrated.
- Being **aggressive** can make others feel angry or intimidated.
- Bring **manipulative** can make others feel powerless or as though they are being taken advantage of.
- Being **assertive** allows others to know where they stand and to feel respected. It also encourages them to be assertive rather than be forced to react to one of the other behaviours.

Do you need to be more assertive? Looking at two main areas may help:

- **why you behave non-assertively**
- **assertiveness techniques.**

11.2.2 Reasons for not behaving assertively

There are many reasons for not behaving assertively, including lack of confidence, thinking that others are better than we are or not knowing what we want. Assertiveness is about thinking *"I'm OK: you're OK"*. (Berne, 1981)

A starting point might be to find out why you tend to behave non-assertively in certain situations and then what you might do about it.

For example if you are **non-assertive:**

- **when you feel negative about something,** you could try to rephrase negative thoughts positively
- **when you are under stress,** you could identify what causes the stress and see if you can take action to reduce it
- **because you are trying to please others,** you could begin to think also about **your own** needs.

Reasons for non-assertive behaviour	Possible solutions

NOTES

Sometimes people behave non-assertively because they have never considered the alternative. The following "bill of rights" may help here:

I have the right to:

1   express my thoughts and opinion
2   express my feelings and be responsible for them
3   say "yes" to people
4   change my mind without making excuses
5   make mistakes and be responsible for them
6   say "I don't know"
7   say "I don't understand"
8   ask for what I want
9   say "no" without feeling guilty
10   be respected by others and respect them
11   be listened to and taken seriously
12   be independent
13   be successful
14   choose not to assert myself.

From Townend (1991)

Which of the above do you find difficult to claim? What can you do to remedy these?

"Rights" I find difficult to claim	Actions to take

11.2.3 Goals and needs

If you are to behave assertively, you must know what you need and want to happen. For a situation currently facing you, can you identify your needs and goals?

My needs	My goals

Being assertive involves acknowledging that others have needs and goals and that solutions have to be found which are acceptable to all parties. What are the needs and goals of the others involved?

Their needs	Their goals

11.2.4 Assertiveness techniques

Being assertive is partly about attitudes and partly about how we behave. If we begin to behave in a way which is assertive, even if we don't feel assertive, it starts to "rub off", builds confidence and can make us feel different. The following techniques can help.

We use as an example the group work scenario given in Section 11.1.2 above. In this scenario "A" should have produced a graph for a group project but has not done so.

"Broken record"

This technique involves repeating what you want without becoming drawn into an argument.

Statement	Response
"You agreed to produce a graph, and we need it for our presentation tomorrow."	*"I haven't got time."*
"Yes, but we need it for tomorrow."	*"I've had a lot of other things to do."*
"I appreciate that, but the presentation is tomorrow."	*"Can't somebody else do it?"*
"We agreed that you would do it, and tomorrow is the deadline."	*"OK, I'll do it tonight."*

If you do get drawn into an argument you are lost.

For example:

Statement	Response
"I haven't got time."	*"You've had as much time as us."*
"No I haven't."	*"Yes you have."* And so on.

Acknowledging criticisms

Accepting criticisms, but without grovelling, can defuse matters.

For example:

"That's right I should have produced the graph."

Accepting compliments

Learn to accept compliments without putting yourself down.

For example:

Statement	Response
"That graph looks good."	*"Thanks"* **not** *"It's not as neat as I wanted!"*

Asking for clarification

If others criticise in a vague way, ask them to be specific. **For example:** *"How have I not pulled my weight?"*

Avoiding preambles

Long preambles to a simple request or statement can confuse the listener and weaken the statement. **For example:** *"We don't want to trouble you, and I know you are very busy, and there was the concert, and I know you've had a cold, but please could you do the graph?"*

It is better to make a direct request. **For example:** *"Could you do the graph please?"*

Acknowledging and recognising your feelings

It is important to recognise your feelings. What was your initial gut reaction to being asked to do something? Pleasure? Panic? What do those initial feelings tell you that you should do? If the feeling was pleasure, this may confirm that it was the right thing to do. If it was panic, you may need to consider whether to refuse the request or ask for more details or for help.

"Going up the gears"

If you don't get what you want the first time become increasingly firm, as opposed to starting off at a maximum position. **For example:**

- **First ask where the graph is.**
- **Make it clear when it is needed by.**
- **Ask what the problem is.**
- **Firmly ask "A" to do it.**
- **Refer the matter to the lecturer if the request is refused.**

Being aware of your appearance

Dressing well can increase your confidence.

Non-verbal signals send messages to the other person about how you feel. Some non-verbal behaviour makes you look assertive – eg if you face the other person on the same level (if the other person stands while you sit they may appear dominant).

Examples of non-assertive non-verbal behaviours:

- **stooped posture**
- **no eye contact**
- **a soft, angry or loud voice**
- **gestures, such as pointing fingers and biting nails.**

Examples of assertive, non-verbal behaviours:

- **upright posture**
- **eye contact**
- **firm clear voice**
- **relaxed gestures.**

Practising saying "no"

Practise saying "no" without excuses. It will get easier. For example: *"I'm afraid I'm busy on Tuesday evening"*, not *"I'm really sorry but I've got an essay to write, and I need to ring Mum, and I've got to wash my socks, and…"*

NOTES

11.3 JUDGING YOUR EFFECTIVENESS

How effective are you at meeting your own goals and needs and allowing for those of others? Are you negotiating effectively? Are you being assertive? The following can help you monitor and review what is happening.

What I did	Effect on me	Effect on others	Changes needed

11.4 REFERENCES AND BIBLIOGRAPHY

Libraries may have materials on this skill area. The following give examples:

Berne, E. (1981) *Games People Play: The Psychology of Human Relationships*, Castle.

Dickson, A. (1982), *A Woman in Your Own Right*, Quartet Books.

Fisher, R. and Ury, W. (1987), *Getting to Yes. How to Negotiate to Agreement Without Giving In*, Arrow Books.

Moores, R. (1989), *Negotiating Skills*, Industrial Society.

Scott, B. and Billing, B. (1990), *Negotiating Skills in Engineering and Construction*, Thomas Telford.

Steele, P., Murphy, J., and Russill, R. (1989), *It's a Deal: A Practical Negotiation Handbook*, McGraw-Hill.

Townend, A. (1991), *Developing Assertiveness*, Routledge.

NOTES

12 COPING WITH PRESSURE

by Sue Drew and Rosie Bingham

CONTENTS

Being under pressure carries both advantages and dangers. Human beings respond to, and are encouraged by, challenges, and a certain amount of tension is positive. The great advances in civilisation have been made by individuals dealing with and overcoming challenges or problems.

However, the human body's biochemical processes respond to a challenge or threat by releasing noradrenalin – the "fight or flight" hormone – into the bloodstream. Modern society's rules of behaviour often prevent us from fighting or fleeing, so there is no release of physical tension. Unrelieved tension causes stress. We all experience stress and deal more or less effectively with it.

Certain illnesses can be stress-related – eg heart disease and high blood pressure. Long before we reach that extreme stage stress can impair our performance.

People react to stress differently but common **psychological** responses include: changes in sleep patterns; irritability; loss of temper; excessive worrying. Common **physical** symptoms of stress include: minor stomach ailments; shallow breathing; minor illnesses such as sore throats or more serious ones such as ulcers.

If you are not sleeping well, are falling out with those around you or taking days off sick, you will not be able to get the most out of studying and enjoying life at university or college.

We suggest you use this SkillPack:

- **when a period of pressure is approaching (eg exams)**
- **when you are in a difficult situation**
- **to handle ongoing course pressures.**

You may also find if helpful to talk to others about this SkillPack.

When you have completed it, you should be able to:

1 identify, by seeking feedback from others, your own reactions and usual responses to pressure
2 identify sources of pressure
3 evaluate the effectiveness of your own reactions and responses, and identify needs for change
4 plan short-term goals related to needs for change, and plan actions needed
5 identify and use sources of support
6 put plans into action, record and review progress.

You should be able to use these elements of the skill on your course or programme with feedback and support from other students, lecturers or tutors and university or college support agencies.

12.1 SOURCES OF PRESSURE AND STRESS

NOTES

Different people react differently to pressure and even have different views on what causes it – eg some students positively enjoy exams while others are unable to think straight in them. It is our perception of our ability to cope in a given situation that matters, not the situation itself.

Excessive stress may be caused by one or two major occurrences or by a cluster of small ones.

Generally we feel stressed by: things which are very important to us; changes which impose new pressures; continually facing situations or people we don't know how to handle.

Any change in general life events – even welcome ones – can be stressful. The table overleaf gives some indication of the wide range of stressors in our lives. Those at the top of each section have the highest impact on our stress levels.

Look through the list and add your own experiences of the events or situations in the right hand column, where you feel it appropriate – eg getting a place on an HE course, leaving home for the first time, making new friends, coping with examinations, going for placement interviews etc.

Events/experiences	My stressors (experienced within the past year)
Relationships	
Death of a partner	
Divorce/separation/break-up of relationship	
Death of a close family member/friend	
Marriage	
Marital reconciliation	
Sex difficulties	
Children leaving home	
Difficulties with relatives	
Partner starts/stops work	
Making new friends	
Prison term	
Personal injury/illness	
Pregnancy	
Outstanding personal achievement	
Change in living conditions	
Moving house/finding lodgings	
Change in recreation activities (eg sport)	
Change in personal habits (eg sleeping/eating)	
Holiday/Christmas	
Loss of job (eg dismissal/redundancy), retirement	
Balancing work and study	
Change in work (eg different work, responsibilities, work load)	
Begin or end school/college	
Difficulties with work	
Change in work hours or conditions	
Change in financial state	
Large mortgage, debts, no grant	
Foreclosure of mortgage or loan	
Small mortgage or loan	

Use the following to make notes on your current pressures – eg on your course or in your life at university or college or outside:

NOTES

On my course or in my life at University or College or outside what is particularly important to me at the moment?

What do other people want from me and who wants it?

What is happening that is new or different in my life?

Has my workload or level of activities changed?

Are there people who upset or annoy me? Why?

Do I experience stress symptoms in particular situations?

NOTES

12.2 IDENTIFYING YOUR OWN REACTIONS TO PRESSURE/SIGNS OF STRESS

In what positive ways do you tend to react to pressure? It is worth reminding yourself of your strengths. How will you know if you are reacting negatively and feeling stressed? It is worth being able to identify the signs so that you can take remedial action.

12.2.1 Positive reactions to pressure

Add your own items to the following checklist.

✔

When under pressure I...	
think more clearly	
work faster	
discard or ignore what is unimportant	
take a step back and think before acting	
see the pressure as an opportunity	
see the pressure as a challenge	
enjoy meeting targets	

12.2.2 Stress – negative reactions to pressure

✔

NOTES

How often do you:	Often	Some-times	Rarely	Never
feel irritable?				
feel restless?				
feel angry?				
feel frustrated at having to wait for something?				
talk fast?				
walk fast?				
feel rushed?				
slump?				
become easily confused?				
have memory problems?				
find it difficult to concentrate?				
think about negative things without wanting to?				
have marked mood swings?				
feel weepy?				
smoke?				
drink alcohol?				
eat too much?				
eat when you are not hungry?				
go off your food?				
not have enough energy to get things done?				
wake up early?				
find it difficult to fall asleep?				
find it difficult to get out of bed in the morning?				
feel you can't cope?				
find it hard to make decisions?				
feel sorry for yourself?				
worry about the future?				
feel you have lost your sense of humour?				
take tranquillisers?				
take non-prescribed drugs?				
have minor accidents?				
have emotional outbursts?				
generally feel upset?				

NOTES

We all feel or do most of these things from time to time, but if most of your ticks are in the "often" or "sometimes" columns it might be time to review your lifestyle. It is easy to fall into destructive behavioural habits, accept them as "normal" and fail to realise that they are indicators of stress which can be removed or reduced.

How many ticks did you have in the "Sometimes" column?	How many ticks did you have in the "Often" column?

When you are stressed what are the most significant signs for you?

12.2.3 How are you reacting to current pressures?

How are you reacting to current pressures and what are the advantages or disadvantages? For example, putting things off may make you feel better in the short term but can cause longer-term problems. You may find it helpful to discuss with friends how they think you react to pressure. What advantages or disadvantages can they see in your reactions?

Source of pressure	My reaction	Advantages	Disadvantages

NOTES

12.3 HOW CAN YOU COPE WITH PRESSURE?

The following suggests a range of helpful strategies. Some of these may suit some situations better than others – you need to pick and choose. You could refer back to your notes on current pressures (Section 1).

12.3.1 Remove the cause of the pressure

You could remove yourself from the situation – eg if you live in a shared flat and can't work because of others' noise you could move out and find other quieter flatmates, or live alone.

However, sometimes it may be better in the long term to stay and sort the problem out, and you may not be able to escape from certain situations easily.

12.3.2 Find a better way of dealing with the pressure

What could you do differently? For example:

- **Be clearer about what you want** and tell people in an assertive way (see chapter on "Negotiating and Assertiveness").

- **Prepare.** If you've got an interview think it through in advance; if you've got an exam, plan your revision (use "Revising and Examination Techniques", see Contents); if you have been "last minuting", forward planning might help (see chapter on "Organising Yourself and Your Time").

- **Take a fresh look at the situation.** Write the problem down, list the options, then think about the alternative approaches (see chapter on "Solving Problems").

- **Talk the situation over with someone else** to help clarify things.

12.3.3 Keep fit

You are more likely to cope if you feel well. Regular exercise can use up "fight or flight" hormones, and it does not have to be strenuous – little and often is the key. Making short journeys on foot instead of catching the bus may make the difference between feeling tense and relaxed.

Eat healthily – there is evidence that certain foods cause stress. The healthy diet advocated nowadays comprises lots of fruit and vegetables and less "junk food".

It may not feel like it at the time, but drinking alcohol and smoking increase stress. They are stimulants which add to the agitation caused by the "fight or flight" hormones.

12.3.4 Put things into perspective

What is the worst that could happen? How likely is this, and how important would it be in six months' or a year's time?

Are there positive consequences? Humour is therapeutic – can you laugh things off?

12.3.5 Treat the symptoms of stress

Some simple techniques can reduce the symptoms of stress.

Breathing exercises
If you are anxious you may tend to breathe shallowly, only using the top of your lungs. Breathe fully out, pulling your stomach in. Then breathe in by letting your stomach out, allowing air to fill the bottom of your lungs. Breathe out to a count of 4, 6 or 8 and in to the same count. This technique should control butterflies in your stomach and calm you and nobody will know you are doing it.

Relaxation exercises
Lie down or sit in a comfortable chair. In turn, tense and then relax your muscles. Start with your foot, then your calf muscles, and move up through the whole body, finally relaxing the facial muscles and the scalp.

Think about something pleasant – a holiday location or a room you like. See it with your "mind's eye" and concentrate on it.

If you can't sleep, count backwards aloud from 500 to stop your mind racing. Keep a pad by the bed and write down what you are thinking.

Other forms of relaxation include meditation, massage and yoga. There are plenty of yoga classes around, and being in a group can make it easier to become involved.

12.3.6 Seek help

If you feel under stress you could seek help. For example:

- **Consult friends:** "a problem shared is a problem halved".

- **Join others with similar concerns:** you may find lists of groups in the students' union or library or you could form one yourself (mature students'/women's/gay groups, etc).

- **Consult your tutor/lecturer:** s/he may help you understand a subject better, or plan your time more effectively.

- **Take a study skills course:** this may reduce fear of exams or other coursework.

- **Consult the Careers Services:** they can help you consider your work options at the end of your course, or help with interview and self-presentation techniques.

- **Consult a counselling service:** this can provide support and an opportunity to talk things through.

- **Join in recreational activities:** many universities and colleges have Recreation Services which provide sports activities (at "competitive" and "fun" levels).

- **Visit your Medical Centre/doctor:** this can help if the symptoms have made you ill, or help you to prevent them making you ill.

- **Join an appropriate support group:** eg if you are disabled, your university or college may have a special unit to provide support.

12.4 WHAT YOU CAN DO DIFFERENTLY

It could help to review this SkillPack and your notes on it, to summarise the main areas you want to change, what actions you could take and who or what might help. Use the chart below.

Areas to change	Actions to take	Sources of help

12.5 REFERENCES AND BIBLIOGRAPHY

Libraries may have materials on this skill area. The following give examples:

Atkinson, J. M. (1988), *Coping with Stress at Work*, Thorsons Publishers.

Cooper, C., Cooper, R. and Eaker, L. (1988), *Living with Stress*, Penguin.

Farmer, R., Monahan, L. and Hekeler, R. (1984), *Stress Management for Human Services*, Sage Publications.

Fontana, D. (1989), *Problems in Practice – Managing Stress*, The British Psychological Society and Routledge.

Looker, T. and Gregson, O. (1989), *Stresswise*, Hodder & Stoughton.

Patel, C. (1989), *The Complete Guide to Stress Management*, Optima.

13
REVISING AND EXAMINATION TECHNIQUES

by Sue Drew and Rosie Bingham

CONTENTS

Examinations are a common form of assessment. If you have entered university or college straight from school you are likely to have considerable experience of them — less so if you are a more mature student, or from a BTEC course where you may have been assessed differently (eg through course work or phase tests).

Whatever your background, university or college exams may differ from those you have experienced to date, as may the type and amount of material to be revised.

Given the importance of exams for most final qualifications, it is well worth considering how to improve your performance.

Even if exams in the early stages of your course do not count towards final grades, they are important in helping you develop your revision and exam techniques. It is helpful to have developed effective strategies before your final exams.

If you have a disability which may affect your exam performance, speak to your lecturer as early as possible about alternative arrangements.

We suggest you use this SkillPack:

- **when you have an exam coming up, to help you plan the revision for it and then to perform successfully in it.**

When you have completed it, you should be able to:

1 identify the purpose and format of the examination and what the examiners are seeking
2 identify which material to revise
3 identify, from a range of revision techniques, which ones are best suited to yourself, the material and the format of the exam
4 plan actions and the time required for revision, within given constraints
5 monitor progress and amend plans
6 identify your own usual reactions and responses to the examination situation, and plan for them
7 identify what the question means and analyse what is required
8 identify which questions to answer in which order and plan time allocation
9 plan answers which include appropriate evidence
10 review your own revision and examination strategies and identify improved methods for the future.

You should be able to use the above elements of the skill on your course, with guidance and support from your tutors.

13.1 YOUR CURRENT EXPERTISE

Think about the last exam(s) you took.

- **Did you do as well as you deserved?**
- **What did you do which worked well/less well?**

In the following box, please focus on how you carried out your revision and how you handled the exam, rather than on how well you dealt with the subject matter.

Revision	
What I did well: *eg started to revise early*	**What I did less well:** *eg didn't manage to cover all the subjects in the time I allowed*

The exam itself	
What I did well: *eg answered all the questions*	**What I did less well:** *eg answered the best question last*

It might help to discuss your replies with (an)other student(s). What did they do which was different from what you did? You can then consider:

- **what aspects of your revising and exam techniques are effective and can be built on**
- **what aspects of your revising and exam techniques are not effective and need improvement.**

13.2 WHAT IS THE EXAM FOR?

In order to revise and then to perform well in the exam it helps to identify what the examiner is looking for. This may vary from subject to subject and also between levels in a subject – eg between years 1 and 2.

In the following box tick what you think was looked for in the exams for a subject which you studied in the past, and then what you think the examiner will look for in your next exams.

✔

What did/will the examiner look for?	GCSE (or similar)	A level, BTEC, Access, profes-sional	This course
The amount of work you have done			
The amount you can write in a given time			
How you cope with the pressure of the exam			
The factual information you know			
How well you grasp what the exam question is aiming at			
Accuracy			
Your writing style – eg spelling, grammar, how you express yourself			
Ability to apply conventions – eg correct references, ways of presenting graphs or diagrams, use of scientific terms			
The presentation of your exam paper			
Being able to apply knowledge to a particular situation			
The underlying concepts/principles you know			
Being able to argue a particular point of view			
Being able to criticise and analyse information			
Other(s) (make a list):			

If you are unsure how to complete the final column of the above box in relation to your current course you can:

• **look at previous exam papers.** You may find examples in university or college libraries, in your course/programme guide or by asking your lecturer.

What does **the format** suggest about what they are looking for? For example, many short questions may mean that knowledge of factual information is required, or a case study may mean that ability to apply knowledge to a particular situation is being tested.

What do **the type of questions** suggest about what they are looking for? For example, do the questions ask you to repeat the knowledge you have or to do something with it (eg to present two sides of an argument, to analyse etc)?

- **ask your lecturer what is expected both by her/himself or by an external examiner.** In all courses and programmes exam results are approved by an exam board attended by your lecturers and an external examiner, usually a lecturer from another university or college.

It is worth checking out your assumptions. For example, in universities or colleges the examiners will not be as concerned with how much you write in a given time as with **what** you write.

13.3 WHAT SHOULD YOU REVISE?

How can you choose what to revise? This may depend partly on:

- **what is likely to be covered in the exam**
- **what will maximise your marks.**

What do your responses to Section 13.2, "What is the exam for?", imply about choosing what to revise? Have the selection methods you have used in the past worked? What are their advantages and disadvantages?

- **How do you normally choose?**
- **Which other methods could you try instead?**

Selection method	In the past	Could try
Work through the material from beginning to end and try to cover it all		
Cover all the material to some extent but identify particular areas to focus on		
Focus on topics which seem difficult		
Focus on topics which seem interesting or easy		
Look at previous exam papers to identify what might crop up		
Ask the lecturer what is critical and likely to crop up		
Memorise as much factual information as possible		
Focus on the main principles/concepts		
Focus on the main principles/concepts and also the factual information which provides evidence for them		
Base your selection on the format of the exam – eg will you only have to answer three long questions on three topics or 50 short questions on a wide range of topics?		
Others. Please specify:		

NOTES

13.4 WHAT REVISION TECHNIQUES CAN YOU USE?

13.4.1 What helps people remember?

The best revision techniques are **active**. Just reading through notes is insufficient to make you remember them. Even if you could recite them word for word, it is unlikely to be enough. In university or college you rarely have to just repeat information in an exam; you must also demonstrate that you can use it in some way.

People are more likely to remember something if:

- **it is relevant to them.** How can you make the material more relevant to you? *eg see revision technique (e) below*

- **it is associated with something else** (just as we remember a person's name by remembering where we met). *eg see revision techniques (f), (h) below*

- **they remember things in sequence,** so that one thing triggers the next element (like an actor's/actress's cue). *eg see revision technique (k) below*

- **they do something with the information.** All the following suggestions involve actively doing something.

13.4.2 Suggestions for revision techniques

You could consider which of the following revision techniques are best suited to the subject and form of the exam (so you need information about the exam well in advance), as well as to your own way of working.

a) Before you start revising, sort out your material for each subject so that you know how much and what material you have. This will help you to plan your revision.

b) Try to keep notes and other materials well organised. Final revision is easier if you go through your material each week, making notes clearer, putting in headings and checking on what you don't understand. Use different coloured pens for different topics, highlighting pens, or coloured dividers in files. See chapter on "Note Taking" for ideas on how to improve your notes.

c) Try to identify the central questions at the heart of each subject and plan how you would answer them.

d) Test yourself. Look at some material and subsequently jot down what you can recall. Then go back to the original material and see what you remembered.

Look at some material and write down some questions on it. Leave it for a few days, then try to answer the questions and "mark" yourself.

e) When you recall your material, try to link the topic with other elements on your course, rather than revising as if the subjects are unrelated.

Produce a card for each topic with notes about other topics it refers to.

f) Use patterns. Write a theme word on a page and connect it through lines to related topics. This can be more memorable than a list because it has visual impact. You can practise reproducing it from memory and modify it as the connections become clearer in your mind. If, in the exam, a question contains one of the words in the pattern you could reproduce the image in rough as a starting point.

g) Look at a section of the material and jot down a summary of the main points. Keep the summaries to use as a brief reminder.

h) Flash cards. Read through your notes, make summaries for each topic and then further reduce them to a few words on a card. As the exam approaches, reading through the flash cards can serve as a quick reminder.

i) Work with a friend. Test each other on factual information. Summarise for each other a topic you have just revised. Explain a difficult concept to a friend and check that s/he understands what you mean. Discuss what questions might crop up and how you might answer them.

j) If you don't understand your material when you come to revise, try to clarify it. Use the library. Ask friends, the lecturer or tutor.

k) For science, technology or quantitative subjects, go back over tutorial sheets and assignments and work again through the calculations or problems, to ensure you understand each stage and can use the techniques. Practising using techniques in advance will make you more aware of which ones to apply to problems presented in exams, and will help you to use them accurately.

l) Make lists – eg of important sequences, or vital points, or steps in a process, or authors etc.

m) Practise in advance. Think of likely questions and make outlines of how to answer them. Try to answer previous papers in the time allowed; identify likely questions and practise producing a reply.

n) Record information on tape and listen to it while driving or cooking.

o) Ask friends how they revise. They may have useful suggestions.

p) Try to understand your own capacities for concentration. How long can you concentrate for? Build in breaks. The above techniques should help you concentrate, as they involve doing something.

Being tired or hungry can affect you. If you are distracted by a thought (what to have for tea, somebody you need to phone), write it down, put it to one side and look at it later. If your mind wanders you may need to stop for a while. Revising different subjects on the same day might add variety.

q) What environment do you work best in? Quiet? With or without music? Warm? Cold? Alone? With others? How could you create that environment? Where could you work?

r) Revising is hard work. Give yourself treats.

NOTES

NOTES

You could note below the ideas which you intend to use:

Revision techniques to use

13.5 PLANNING YOUR REVISION

13.5.1 How much time have you got to revise?

Many people put off revising and panic when they realise time is running out. Panic can mean you think less clearly, and it interferes with memory. Identify what you could do in advance. The following is an example only. A blank revision plan is given in Section 13.5.4 for you to use.

2 months in advance	Sort out notes, ensuring that they are understandable
1 month in advance	Make summaries of notes
1 week in advance	Test self
1 day in advance	Use flash cards

13.5.2 Make a plan

A major difference between university or college and school is that you are seen as being more responsible for your own learning. Lecturers assume that you will decide for yourself what to revise, how and when. You may receive very little direction about this. An important educational aim is to encourage students to be independent.

A plan might include what you are going to revise, how and when. Listing the topics you need to revise within each subject/unit means you can tick them off as you go along. You could produce a day-by-day revision timetable. A plan can:

- **indicate if you are spending too much time on one subject**
- **alert you to what still needs to be done**
- **serve as a psychological boost by showing what you have already done.**

Section 13.5.4 below includes a possible layout for such a plan.

13.5.3 Coping with pressure

You need a balance between revision and the rest of your life.

You need breaks, exercise, variety, to keep in touch with friends and family.

You are more likely to cope with pressure if you are physically fit and keep things in perspective – see chapter on "Coping with Pressure".

What other demands on your time exist? Could you plan ahead to create some space near to the exams? If you produce a day-by-day revision timetable, you can build in breaks and make sure that you take them.

NOTES

13.5.4 Revision plan

Subject/what to revise	Revision techniques	By when? – deadline	Progress/notes of further action needed

13.6 TAKING EXAMS

Think about the last exam you sat:

How did you spend the first 10 minutes of it? What did you do?

How did you feel during the first 10 minutes?

What did you do during the middle part of the exam?

What did you do during the last 10 minutes?

How did you feel during and at the end of the exam?

Section 13.7 should help you focus on what you can do in your external exam to build on strengths and improve on weaker areas.

13.7 EXAM TECHNIQUES

13.7.1 Types of examinations

An unseen exam

This is any exam where you do not know what it will contain in advance.
Examples might be:

Essays/problems

Usually these require you to apply your knowledge to a particular situation – eg to answer a particular problem or to present an argument from a particular standpoint.

Short-answer questions

Here you are given a number of questions which require only a very short answer, often relating to factual knowledge.

Tip. It may be best not to waste time on those you cannot answer. Answer those you can and return to the rest if you have time. Avoid wasting time by giving more information than is asked for. If there are only two marks for an answer you won't get any more by writing more.

Multiple choice

Here you have to choose between several given answers.

Tip. Answer those you are sure of and return to those which require more thought.

Phase tests

These are short tests of usually no more than an hour. They test that students have grasped the essential elements of a specific and small section of material (ie that covered in one "phase" of the course).

A seen exam

This is where you are given material or the questions in advance. The focus is less on remembering information and more on what you do with it – eg analysing it, presenting arguments etc. In seen exams you will generally be expected to provide accurate information and references (as you will not be relying on memory). Examples might be:

Open book exams

Here you can take material into the exam.

Take away

You may be given a question in advance to complete in your own time and return by a given date, or you may be given a question to prepare in advance but answer it under exam conditions (eg in an exam room and within a time limit). One example is where you are given a case study or data in advance, and in an exam situation you are then asked questions based on the case or the data.

13.7.2 Exam techniques

The following cover a range of exam techniques, some of which will be reminders of what you already do, while others will be new to you.

a) If you have a disability which may make it difficult for you to perform well in an exam, you need to bring this to the attention of your lecturer well in advance and discuss any special arrangements which can be made – eg making braille or large-print exam papers available.

b) Arrive at the exam in plenty of time. Arriving late reduces the time you have and may create panic. When you arrive will it help you to chat to others, or will this make you feel anxious? If the latter, wait outside until it is time to go in.

c) Make a list in advance of what you need to take into the exam (eg calculator, spare batteries, pens, pencils etc). Finding in the middle of an exam that you do not have an essential item may cause panic. Check in advance what you are allowed to take with you.

d) Spend five minutes reading the exam paper, deciding which questions to answer. Clarify the instructions, so that you answer the correct number of questions. If you only answer three instead of four, for example, you automatically lose 25%.

e) What do the questions mean? Underline the key words in each question to identify exactly what is being asked. For example:

- *compare/contrast* (implies looking at two or more different perspectives)
- *evaluate* (implies offering criticisms or making judgements)
- *analyse* (implies asking why, looking at two underlying factors)
- *explain* (implies laying out each stage in a process or argument or each aspect of an object in a logical way).

A common reason for losing marks is not answering the question asked. You will get no credit for an answer which is irrelevant even if it is excellent. It is easy to misread things if you are nervous, and it can help to paraphrase the question in your own words, and to keep referring back to it while answering it.

f) Try to avoid questions which contain a word or phrase that you don't understand. If you guess wrongly you may get few marks.

g) Decide how long you will allocate to each question, then monitor your timekeeping. Allow 10 minutes at the end for checking.

h) Spend a few minutes planning your answers. You can jot down notes and then cross them out, so the examiner knows not to assess them. You may get better marks for coherent and logical arguments than a list of ideas on a topic.

i) Where the exam requires essay-type answers, aim to write a strong introductory paragraph showing that you understand the question and a strong last one where you draw conclusions, returning to the question asked. This will demonstrate to the examiner that your answer is purposeful and relevant.

j) The first 50% of marks for a question is the easiest to obtain. The next 25% is harder. The last 25% is very difficult to achieve. If you are running out of time, two half answers may be worth more than one whole.

eg $^{15}/_{25} + {}^{15}/_{25} + {}^{12}/_{25} + {}^{10}/_{25}$

is better than

$^{20}/_{25} + {}^{18}/_{25} + {}^{10}/_{25} + {}^{1}/_{25}$

If you do overrun the time you have allocated for a question, jot down rough notes of the main points you still need to include while they are fresh in your mind and move on to the next question. If you have time you can return to it later.

k) Write clearly! A model answer will gain no marks if the examiner cannot read it. Examiners are influenced by how well work is presented (imagine marking 100 exam scripts). Make sure you number your answers correctly, especially if you do them out of sequence.

l) At university or college, answers are expected to show a rigorous understanding of the subject. Avoid unsupported opinions and include evidence to demonstrate your points. Unless specifically asked for, this will usually not mean personal experiences, but rather evidence from research or from the literature on the subject.

m) Quantity will not gain marks. It is more important to make relevant points than to include irrelevancies or padding. Padding takes valuable time to produce without improving your grade. If you think you have covered all the main points in an answer, move on.

n) You could plan your answers to the second, third, fourth etc questions after you have finished your first answer. At this stage you are over the initial tension of the exam, but you still have time for planning – time which you may run out of as the exam progresses.

o) Spend the last 10 minutes checking your work – eg how you have numbered your answers, spelling, handwriting, ensuring that all the steps have been shown in a calculation etc.

p) If you are used to short exams, such as phase tests, and you now face a long exam (eg three hours), reconsider the above suggestions and think what you will need to do differently. For example, in a long exam you have more discretion to decide how to use your time, so you may need to pay more attention to spending the first 5-10 minutes of the exam in planning.

13.8 COPING WITH EXAM NERVES

Exams are stressful – but stress is not necessarily negative. You are more mentally alert under stress, which is why you can produce so much in the short space of an exam. Research indicates that you will perform better if you view stress as positive and exams as a chance to demonstrate your abilities rather than as a way of tripping you up.

- A lot of anxiety can be reduced by good preparation, and by sufficient revision to make you feel confident.

- Make sure you know: when and where the exam will be; how long it will be; how many questions there are; how much choice there is; what the arrangements are if you want to go to the toilet, or if you have a problem during the exam (like a calculator breaking down, for example).

- It can help to find out in advance from the lecturer the criteria against which the exam will be assessed. Do all the exam questions carry equal marks? What percentage of the overall mark does it represent? What happens if you are ill or if you fail?

- It can help to reduce anxiety if you spend the first 10 minutes in an exam planning how to deal with it and then try to stick to the plan. It avoids the "flitting about" or "getting stuck" that nerves sometimes induce.

- Some people like to swap their experiences with others after an exam and find it releases tension. This can be helpful in acknowledging that most people experience exam nerves, and in discussing how to avoid problems.

  Others may find this makes them more anxious. If the latter applies to you, leave as soon as possible after the exam.

- Ways of coping with stress include yoga, relaxation, avoiding too much alcohol and leading a generally healthy lifestyle in terms of food and exercise. See chapter on "Coping with Pressure".

13.9 IMPROVING YOUR REVISION AND EXAM TECHNIQUES

After the exam it should help to complete the following. This can be the start of your preparation for your next one.

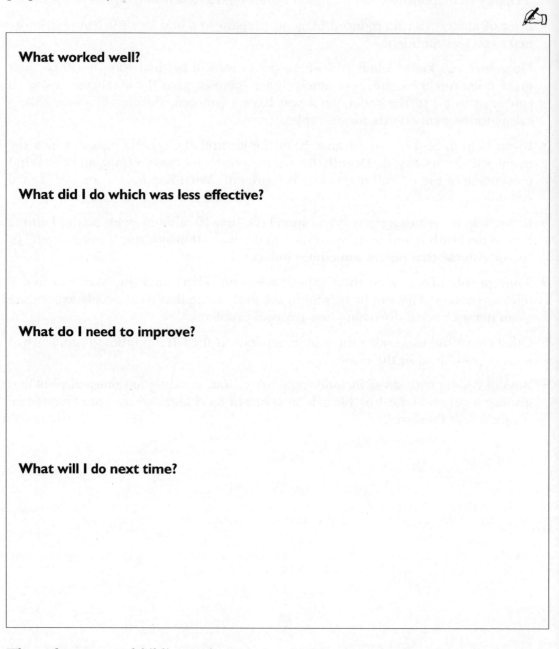

What worked well?

What did I do which was less effective?

What do I need to improve?

What will I do next time?

The references and bibliography (Section 13.10) gives details of materials which might help you. Check whether your university or college runs study skills courses.

13.10 REFERENCES AND BIBLIOGRAPHY

Libraries may have materials on this skill. The following give examples:

Books and written material

Acres, D. (1982), *How to Pass Exams Without Anxiety*, How To Books, Hamlyn.

Buzan, T. (1973), *Use Your Head*, BBC Publications.

Coles, M. and White, C. (1992), *How to Study and Pass Exams*, Collins.

Gibbs, G. (1981), *Teaching Students to Learn*, Open University Press.

Habeshaw, S., Habeshaw, J. and Gibbs, G. (1987), *53 Interesting Ways of Helping Your Students to Study*, Technical and Educational Services Limited.

Jacques, D. (1990), *Studying at the Polytechnic*, Education Methods Unit, Oxford Polytechnic.

National Extension College (1994), *Learning Skills*, Units 42-50 National Extension College.

Northedge, A. (1990) *The Good Study Guide*, Open University Press.

Videos

Secrets of Study – Interactive Video. Mast Learning Systems, 1989.

PART II

DEVELOPMENT LEVEL SKILLPACKS

14
IDENTIFYING STRENGTHS AND IMPROVING SKILLS

by Sue Drew and Rosie Bingham

CONTENTS

It is not easy to judge our own performance. Often we prefer to get on with a task rather than to think how we are doing so. On courses and in professional life, giving attention to how you do something can improve the result.

Identifying strengths and improving skills is part of the "continuous professional development" regarded as vital by many professional bodies.

Identifying strengths is crucial in applying for placements or for jobs – employers want to know not only what you have done, but how well, and what you are capable of.

This SkillPack assumes that you have some experience of identifying the level of your skills in order to improve your performance. If not you should first read the equivalent SkillPack in Part I. This Development SkillPack focuses more on improving your skills.

You should use this SkillPack:

- **to identify your current skills and their level – our skill levels change continually**
- **to identify the skills you need**
- **to identify how to continuously improve your performance**
- **to identify other chapters in this book which could help you.**

When you have completed it, you will be able to:

1 identify your own strengths and weaknesses, based on appropriate evidence
2 identify development needs, set targets for improving skill areas, and review and revise those targets according to changing circumstances
3 actively seek and use feedback constructively and regularly
4 select activities to improve skill performance which are appropriate to your own strengths and weakness and to the circumstances
5 acknowledge your own responsibility for skill development, whilst seeking and using appropriate support.

You should be able to use this skill on your course/programme and on work placement or in a professional area, with some support from tutors/lecturers, and with feedback from tutors/lecturers, other students, employers or outside contacts.

14.1 YOUR CURRENT SKILLS AND THOSE YOU NEED

This SkillPack assumes that, although there are sources of help and support, it is up to you to identify what you wish to improve and then to take action. It is important to begin by identifying your current skills.

14.1.1 A starting point

It is easier to identify your current level of a skill if you think about it in relation to a particular activity. If you feel uncertain about this process, look at the equivalent SkillPack in Part I before proceeding.

We suggest you:

- **identify the activities likely to be encountered on your course** (this may include class activities, or assessed work such as projects or a dissertation)
- **identify activities you may encounter in the job area you may enter.** If you have no clear idea about the profession you wish to enter, we suggest you think of activities likely to occur in any job (eg attending meetings, meeting deadlines, writing letters/reports etc) or activities you would like as part of a job (eg practical activities, managing others etc).

You can then consider your skills and how to improve them in relation to those course and job activities.

Course activities	Job activities

14.1.2 Diagnosing your needs

The following Diagnosis Sheet will help you identify:

- **which skills you need for your course and any job area you may enter**
- **your current level of skill. Identifying strengths can be a real confidence booster**
- **where you want to improve. Identifying areas which need improvement is an important preliminary.**

Please use the first column on the Diagnosis Sheet to list the skills you need to focus on.

The following is a list of skills covered by other chapters in this book. You could use this list to select skills to consider, and could also add other skills important for your course or for prospective job activities.

Coping with pressure
Gathering and using information
Group work
Negotiating and assertiveness
Note taking
Oral presentation
Organising yourself and your time
Essay writing
Report writing
Revising and examination techniques
Solving problems

In the following columns of the Diagnosis Sheet please consider your need for these skills, or any other skills you identify, in relation to the course/job activities you identified in Section 14.1.1 above, and then identify your current skill level. How well have you used that skill in course (or job) activities up to now? How much are you likely to need it in future?

In the final column identify which skills you most need to improve. For example, where the skill will not be needed to a great extent either in the course or future jobs, it may be a low priority for your attention, even if your current level of the skill is low.

On the other hand, you may be quite good at a skill, but it is so important for your course or future jobs that you feel you still need to improve it.

NOTES

NOTES

14.1.3 Diagnosis sheet

Skill	Course activities needing this skill	Level needed 1-4 (1 = high)	Job activities needing this skill	Level needed 1-4 (1 = high)	My current skill level 1-4 (1 = high)	Skills needing improvement 1-4 (1 = most important to improve)

Skill	Course activities needing this skill	Level needed 1-4 (1 = high)	Job activities needing this skill	Level needed 1-4 (1 = high)	My current skill level 1-4 (1 = high)	Skills needing improvement 1-4 (1 = most important to improve)

NOTES

NOTES

Skill	Course activities needing this skill	Level needed 1-4 (1 = high)	Job activities needing this skill	Level needed 1-4 (1 = high)	My current skill level 1-4 (1 = high)	Skills needing improvement 1-4 (1 = most important to improve)

NOTES

14.2   IMPROVING YOUR SKILLS

14.2.1 Suggestions for how to improve skills

Ways of doing things differently include:

- **use an alternative strategy, or build on positives** (eg oral presentation: if you are good at visual aids emphasise them – the audience can focus on the visual aids rather than on you)

- **change your attitude** (eg oral presentation: see the audience as on your side/making allowances for nervousness/interested in the topic rather than in you)

- **improve the areas you feel weak in** (eg oral presentation: prepare well, practise in front of friends or on tape, anticipate the questions you will be asked, avoid fidgeting)

- **avoid or minimise situations requiring the skill** (eg oral presentation: avoid jobs that require a great deal of oral presentations). You may also have to assess how important it is to you to be in the situation (eg oral presentation: you may need to do oral presentations for assessment, or a job may have many features you like, but also require oral presentations).

14.2.2 Where can you find help?

- **Other SkillPacks.** Ask your tutor.

- **Feedback from others.** Ask for it to be specific (eg oral presentation: don't ask "Was it OK/not OK?" but "What was OK/not OK about it?"). You could tell friends you are trying to improve a skill and ask for ongoing feedback.

- **Libraries.** There are materials such as books and videos on specific skills – you may find some under the general "study skills" title.

- **Your lecturers/tutors.** They may be able to spend time in class on particular skills.

- **Friends and other students** – either from your year or in later years (where they have experienced the stage you are at). What ideas do they have for improving the skill? Support from others can be very important.

NOTES

14.2.3 Taking action

You have identified skill areas relevant to yourself. It can now help to consider the following questions (in each case an example is given which is related to the skill of making oral presentations).

What do you find easy/like about the skills you have identified. Why? Identify the positives – ie the areas you can build on.

Skill	Enjoy/Like	Why?
eg oral presentation	*eg producing visual aids*	*eg good at identifying main points, good at visual layout*

What do you find difficult/dislike about this/these skills? Why?

Skill	Difficult/dislike	Why?
eg oral presentations	eg feel nervous about dealing with questions	eg in case asked something can't answer

Imagine that your weaker areas are now your strengths. What would you be doing differently? What could you do now to move towards that position?

Skill	What I'd do differently	How to get there	By (deadline)
eg oral presentations	eg answer questions confidently	eg identify possible questions in advance	eg next week

NOTES

NOTES

If you find, when you reach a deadline set for a particular action, that you haven't met it, it can help to ask why.

- **What is preventing you?**
- **Was your deadline or target unrealistic?**
- **Do you need a new approach?**
- **Do you need training or advice?**

Changing the way you do things can be difficult. You might need help and you might need to make allowances for yourself. Acknowledge that it's hard and give yourself credit for how far you **have** got.

Unmet target	Why?	Progress which *has* been made	Further action needed

14.3 REFERENCES AND BIBLIOGRAPHY

Libraries may have materials on this skill. The following give examples:

AGCAS (1992) *Where Next? Exploring your Future*, (a series of booklets) AGCAS.

Booklet 1   "Taking the plunge"
Booklet 2   "Reflections"
Booklet 3   "Sharpening the image"
Booklet 4   "Choices"

AGCAS (1992) *Discovering Yourself. A Self-Assessment Guide for Older Students*, AGCAS.

NOTES

15
ORGANISING YOURSELF AND YOUR TIME

by Sue Drew and Rosie Bingham

CONTENTS

This SkillPack aims to help you to make the most of opportunities by being well organised and using time efficiently.

You can achieve more and your performance on the course is likely to be much better if you are well organised. In addition, employers need employees to prioritise and meet deadlines. This is a skill area they will look for when recruiting graduates or higher diplomates.

If you are well organised, you are more likely to be able to cope with pressure and less likely to succumb to stress.

We suggest you use this SkillPack:

- **in conjunction with course activities**
- **at the beginning of a semester or a busy period, to help you plan and monitor your actions.**

When you have completed it, you will be able to:

1 identify your own current practices in organising yourself and your time, and the strengths and weaknesses of those practices
2 identify aims and targets
3 identify and explore strategies and resources (eg delegation) for organising yourself and your time in order to maximise effectiveness
4 select and use strategies to maximise opportunities to meet aims, targets and deadlines
5 identify and use feedback
6 respond effectively to current pressures and plan ahead to meet future pressures.

You should be able to use this skill on your course/programme, on work placement or in a professional area, when you are faced with an unanticipated situation or where you have several conflicting demands, and little support from others.

15.1 YOUR CURRENT SKILLS

The equivalent SkillPack in Part I covers the elements listed in the box below. How would you rate your current skill level against each item? If you feel you need to improve on any of these areas, you should refer back to that SkillPack. When you complete the table, use a scale where 1 = "very well" and 4 = "needs considerable attention".

✔

	1	2	3	4
Being aware of my strengths/weaknesses in how I currently organise myself/my time.				
Identifying immediate actions and targets.				
Estimating how long work will take/planning ahead.				
Reducing time wasters.				
Meeting deadlines.				
Having a well organised workspace.				
Having easy-to-use filing/recording systems.				

15.2 AIMS, GOALS, TARGETS

15.2.1 Long-term

Good planning means not only dealing with immediate targets, but also identifying more general aims and directions. You can then see how your day-to-day actions match with what you want. Are you putting effort into the right areas? What are your long-term aims? Fill in the box below and add your own items.

✔

A good degree/diploma.	
A higher degree.	
An interesting job.	
A job with power or status.	
A well paid job.	
To pursue particular interests.	
Good relationships, family, friends.	
A balanced life (work/leisure/family).	
Other long-term aims (list):	

NOTES

NOTES

15.2.2 Immediate aims and targets

What immediate targets do you have – or things you must do? How long will each take to achieve? Can each target and task be broken down into more realistic sub-tasks? How long will each sub-task take?

It might help to include not only course targets but others too: domestic; work; social. These may impinge on your course work.

Target/task	Sub-tasks	Deadlines

15.2.3 The relationship between long-term and immediate aims and targets

You could now consider the following questions:

Will my immediate targets/tasks support my long-term aims? Which will support them most?

Which immediate targets/tasks are irrelevant to my long-term aims?

Do I want to reconsider or reprioritise my immediate targets? How?

15.2.4 Realistic targets

Are your targets achievable given the time and resources available?

- **Set realistic small goals and record when you've met them. Unrealistic large goals can cause panic.**
- **You can only do one thing at a time. Has your planning allowed for this?**

15.2.5 Conflicting demands

What if you have conflicting demands – eg you need to do different things at the same time? In this case, you may need to prioritise (see Section 15.3.1) or to identify other ways of meeting one of the demands. Could anybody else do it? Could it be done on a different day? Could it be done in any less time? Could it be done in advance?

15.2.6 Saying "no"

Being unwilling to say "no" to others' requests can increase demands on you enormously. These might include social events which you don't like to turn down, requests for help from other students or the needs of family members. It may be helpful to ask yourself the following questions:

- **Have I got time to do this?**
- **Do I want to do this?**
- **Do I have to do it? Could somebody else do it?**
- **Does it really need to be done?**
- **What would happen if I didn't do it?**

If you find it hard to say "no" the chapters on "Negotiating and Assertiveness" might help (see Contents).

15.3 MAKING THE MOST OF OPPORTUNITIES

15.3.1 Prioritising

Nobody can do everything which comes their way. Effectiveness is improved by deciding what should be done now, what later, and what can be left. It helps to be clear about your aims. This gives a yardstick by which to decide priorities (see Section 15.2).

What are your long-, medium- and short-term priorities? Identifying them may help you plan ahead rather than merely deal with what arises day-to-day, which can lead to feeling out of control. Failing to plan ahead can mean not making new opportunities – eg self-employed people need to allow time to obtain new business as well as to carry out current business.

In prioritising for the long term it can help to identify:

- **what would determine your future**
- **what might influence your future to some extent**
- **what would have little effect on your future**
- **what would have no effect on your future at all.**

In prioritising for the short term it can help to identify what is:

1 urgent and important – do it
2 urgent and not important – do it if you can
3 important but not urgent – start it before it becomes urgent
4 not important and not urgent – don't do it.

NOTES

You could return to the box you completed in Section 15.2.2 and add notes indicating priorities.

However, suppose you have prioritised but still have too much to do in too short a time? Possibilities are:

- **Make a list of what you *must* do.** Estimate against each how long it will take and add on half again (most of us seriously underestimate time needed). If it adds up to more time then you have, reprioritise.
- **Make a list of what is to be done in order of priority.** If, after three days, items are still on the list put them at the top or discard them.

15.3.2 Using resources and delegating

What could make things easier and reduce effort? Possibilities include:

- **use computers to word process** (it is easier to correct work once you can use a keyboard)
- **use computers to create databases so that you can find things more easily**
- **find out what resources exist** – an hour spent doing this could avoid future time wasting. Who would know? Librarians? Computer advisers? Lecturers? Friends?
- **find ways of reducing the time you spend on domestic tasks.**

15.4 DEALING WITH THE UNEXPECTED

What about the sudden crisis, the additional piece of work, the breakdown of equipment? What do you normally do when faced by the unexpected?

Possible strategies are as follows:

- **Build in time for the unexpected. Going for an interview? Allow for the train to be late. Need certain books? Allow time for interlibrary loans. Need to use a computer? Assume there will be a queue.**
- **When estimating how long a task will take always add half on again.**
- **Consider delegating work to somebody else. Who? Why might they agree? What benefits would they get? What could they do? The chapters on "Negotiating and Assertiveness" (see Contents) might help in agreeing matters with others.**
- **Share a task with other students – eg researching information.**
- **Rotate domestic duties.**

What resources or people could help with your current or possible future pressures?
Again, it may help to refer back to Section 15.2.2.

Resources/people	How they might help

NOTES

15.5 CURRENT AND FUTURE PRESSURES

If you organise yourself and your time you will hopefully rarely feel under too much pressure. What do you need to do to improve your organisation of yourself and your time? Which of the ideas in this SkillPack could you try?

Area needing improvement	Actions

If you do feel under pressure, you might find the chapters on "Coping with Pressure" helpful (see Contents).

15.6 REFERENCES AND BIBLIOGRAPHY

NOTES

Libraries may have materials on this skill. The following give examples:

Buzan, T. (1973), *Use your Head*, BBC Publications.

Hopson, B. and Scally, M. (1989), *Time Management: Conquer the Clock*, Lifeskills.

Jacques, D. (1990), *Studying at the Polytechnic*, Educational Methods Unit, Oxford Polytechnic.

Northedge, A. (1990), *The Good Study Guide*, Open University Press.

Stuart, R. R. (1989), *Managing Time*, The Pegasus Programme Understanding Industry Inst.

16
GATHERING AND USING INFORMATION

by Sue Drew, Aileen Wade and Andrew Walker

CONTENTS

Skills in gathering and using information are vital for academic success on your current course, if you wish to study a higher degree, and in future employment. All organisations need to base decisions on accurate and up-to-date information.

This SkillPack assumes you are already competent in the basics of gathering and using information. If this is not the case, refer to the equivalent SkillPack in Part I.

In this SkillPack we use an example to illustrate points: finding information about policies on cigarette smoking.

We suggest you use this SkillPack:

- **in relation to a particular piece of work, such as a project or assignment.**

When you have completed it, you should be able to:

1 find sources of information relevant to and sufficient for the purpose and audience
2 use effective reading and observing strategies – eg skimming, scanning, in-depth reading or viewing
3 identify the meaning of subject-specific terminology as used in the programme units studied and in the professional area
4 identify the main points or issues of relevance to the topic
5 accurately record sources of information
6 identify factors which influence the interpretation of the information, identifying any reasons for bias or distortion.

You should be able to use this skill in your course, on work placement or in professional areas, with clarification from lecturers/tutors, other students, libraries and outside organisations.

16.1 YOUR EXISTING SKILLS

Rate your abilities against each item below using a scale in which 1 = "very good" and 4 = "needs considerable improvement". If you feel you need to reconsider any of the items, refer back to the equivalent SkillPack in Part I.

✔

Basic information skills	1	2	3	4
Analysing the task (your research questions)				
Identifying why you need the information				
Identifying who you need it for				
Identifying when you need it by				
Recording information (your filing and indexing systems, how to cite and reference material)				
Identifying where you might find the information				
Using the information (eg reading techniques for covering a lot of material, knowing when you have enough information, answering your research questions)				
Understanding the terms used				

16.2 UNDERSTANDING TERMINOLOGY

As you progress through your course you are increasingly likely to encounter terminology which is specific to your subject and to your professional area. You may go on placement, do work-related projects or write dissertations on professional issues. Unfamiliar terms might include jargon, slang or professional vocabulary. How can you check on meaning? Possibilities are:

- **general dictionaries/encyclopedias/handbooks/thesaurus (which gives alternatives for a word)**
- **subject-specific dictionaries**
- **reference books – eg *Martindale the Extra Pharmacopoeia* lists pharmaceuticals and their effects (Reynolds, 1993)**
- **lecturers/tutors**
- **Library Information Desk staff**
- **fellow students**
- **work colleagues or supervisors**
- **observation/general reading.**

16.3 RECORDING INFORMATION

You are likely to need more information for a piece of work, eg for a dissertation, in the later rather than the earlier stages of your course. You may also want to use the information for different purposes – eg an essay, a report, an oral or visual presentation, an exhibition or a poster session. In deciding how to record information it is important to ask the following questions:

- **How will I use it?**
- **Do I need it for this assignment only, or might I need it again?**
- **In what form will it be presented?**

When considering how you will use the information, you may wish to refer to the chapters on "Report Writing" and "Oral Presentation" (see Contents).

What the information will be used for (its purpose)

You must also consider the following ethical and legal issues when recording information:

- **Copyright.** How much of the material can you reproduce? Your university or college may produce a leaflet on copyright. Library staff can advise.
- **Plagiarism.** To avoid accusations of copying other people's work, you must acknowledge your sources (see the equivalent SkillPack in Part I).
- **Integrity and reliability.** Is it true? Is it accurate? Who says?

Given the items you identified in the box above, what are the best ways to record your information? Refer back to the equivalent SkillPack in Part I for suggestions on simple manual and computerised storage systems.

You may now like to think about further possibilities – eg, you may wish to transfer information from a database to other computer software packages, such as a word processor or a spreadsheet. This could save considerable time and effort. If in doubt, seek help from library staff, from computer help desks or computer technicians in your university or college.

It is important to examine critically what you are doing.

- **Is your way of recording information efficient?**
- **Are there better methods?**
- **Would it help to use a computer software package? (Will it save time or take more time to set up and use than a manual system?)**
- **Can you find information easily and quickly?**
- **Can you easily put it into new formats (a table, chart or other visual display)?**
- **Is your system cheap and simple?**

You may find it helpful to refer to the chapter on "Note Taking" (see Contents).

Ways in which I can record my information

NOTES

16.4 FINDING INFORMATION

16.4.1 Current skills

How would you rate yourself on the following aspects of information-finding, where 1 = "very good" and 4 = "needs considerable improvement"? Where do your ratings suggest you need to improve? This section covers all these items.

✔

	1	2	3	4
Planning ahead				
Using imaginative approaches to finding sources				
Using initiative in finding information				
Using computers to find information				
Persevering in finding information				
Knowing when you've got enough information				

16.4.2 Planning ahead

Do you plan how long it will take to find the information?

- **If you need to write off for information, allow a minimum of two weeks for replies (include a stamped-addressed envelope).**
- **On average, interlibrary loans take two weeks. If another borrower has the book you want they can keep it for three weeks.**
- **Have you allowed for problems, such as other students having the books you need?**
- **If you are unfamiliar with computerised systems, have you added on time for learning to use them?**

You may find it helpful to refer to the chapters on "Organising Yourself and Your Time" (see Contents).

16.4.3 Using imagination

Using our cigarette smoking example, a standard approach might be to do a library catalogue search under "cigarette smoking".

You could also investigate who would be interested in smoking as an issue and identify where would you find information produced by them.

For example:

Who might be interested in smoking as an issue?	Possible sources of information
Politicians	Hansard, newspapers (also on CD-ROM).
Health Service	Local NHS HQ, leaflets in doctors surgeries, Health Statistics, Medline CD-ROM, ASSIA PLUS CD-ROM, CTI PLUS CD-ROM.
Employers	Employers you've worked for, local Chamber of Commerce.
Trades unions	Directories, Industrial Society, TU offices.
Tobacco manufacturers	Advertising directories, trade directories.
People with tobacco related illnesses, or their relatives	Directory of Pressure Groups, Charities Digest.
Civil liberties groups	Directory of Pressure Groups.
Pubs, transport companies, the fire brigade, etc, etc, etc.	etc, etc, etc.

How could you become more aware of sources of information? Possibilities include:

* **discussing it with friends**
* **being alert to the media (newspapers, TV or radio programmes may spark off ideas)**
* **asking specialists, such as Library Information Desk staff, or lecturers**
* **asking people in relevant outside organisations (if you've worked or been on placement do you have any contacts?).**

16.4.4 Initiative

Being imaginative may not be enough on its own. It is also important to "get up and find it". People can be a great source of information and you may need to talk to them. If you feel hesitant about approaching people, the chapters on "Negotiating and Assertiveness" might help (see Contents).

NOTES

NOTES

16.4.5 Using computers to find information

How would you rate yourself on the following scale, where 1 = "very good" and 4 = "needs considerable improvement"?

✔

	1	2	3	4
Are you confident in using computerised systems such as the library catalogue or other databases? There are a range: bibliographic (eg references to journal articles); full-text (eg a newspaper on a CD-ROM); data (eg financial data about a company).				
Can you carry out more sophisticated and precise database searches (eg searching on dates, or authors, or subjects)?				
Can you link terms (eg searching by author and subject and date)?				
Do you understand the difference between word searching (gives everything where the word appears, whether or not it is the main topic) or subject searching (focuses on the topic and is usually more specific)				
Do you know how to create and store data in files on a formatted floppy disk?				
Other aspects of using computers to find information. Please list.				

The above exercise should help you identify what you need to do better. Sources of help include:

- **Library Information Desk staff**
- **friends and other students**
- **lecturers (especially those teaching IT)**
- **library information skills sessions or workshops (ask the Library Information Desks for details).**

16.4.6 Perseverance and knowing when to stop

When seeking information are you more likely to:

✔

make a quick search and then give up?	
keep looking until you have every last scrap of information and not know when to stop?	

Finding information is not like using a "one-stop shop", where you get everything you need off the shelf. You need to be a detective and follow up clues – eg a database may provide references to printed articles; you then need to find the articles; and one article may refer to further articles.

If you tend to search for too long and become overwhelmed by information, it helps to be very clear about your research questions. When you feel you can adequately answer them, stop. (If in doubt about your research questions, refer to the equivalent SkillPack in Part I). Being critical and evaluative is important. Ask yourself continually if you really need this information.

You may experience a decreasing rate of return on effort. You may gather a lot of new facts or ideas initially but come to a point when new sources reveal little extra. This may be the time to stop.

Setting realistic deadlines also helps.

Sources to use for my current piece of work	By (give deadline)

16.5 INTERPRETING AND EVALUATING INFORMATION

16.5.1 Your aims

What are you trying to achieve in gathering information for your work ?

✔

Collection of factual information	
Proof of how much work you've done	
Complete coverage of every possibility	
A focus on what is really important	
Proof of an idea or hypothesis	
A criticism of ideas	
An investigation of underlying meanings	
A clarification of your own views	

All these goals are important and their appropriateness may vary with the task. Sometimes you may need to cover every possibility; at other times you may want to focus on a small area. However, for higher-level information skills the abilities to interpret and evaluate information are increasingly important and are expected of students by the end of their courses.

16.5 INTERPRETING AND EVALUATING INFORMATION

16.5.2 Questions to ask

As you gather information, which of the following questions do you normally ask yourself?

✔

What are the essential elements?	
Are there any recurring themes?	
Are there any connections between aspects of the information?	
Is the information accurate? Do figures add up? Are the statistics misleading? (See Huff, 1973.)	
How up-to-date is the information? Is the date important? Has the information been superseded?	
Why was the information originally prepared? Was there a vested interest? What were the underlying assumptions?	
How selective is the coverage? Does it (perhaps deliberately) omit any information?	
What concepts lie beneath the factual information?	
Do you agree/disagree with these concepts? Why?	
What would people unfamiliar with the material ask about it? What will your audience or reader make of it, or not understand?	

Using our cigarette smoking example, a report may be: selective in the information it presents about the dangers, if written by those in favour of smoking; produced before certain medical evidence emerged; influenced by vested interests such as tax revenue. Do statistics on the connections between smoking and health conceal other factors – eg about social class?

16.6 PROVIDING EVIDENCE

By the end of your course you will be expected not only to describe (a theory, a film, an experiment, a concept etc) but to be critical. The previous section considered the questions you might ask in order to critically evaluate information. However, it is not enough to criticise. You have to provide evidence for your criticisms.

The information you gather is your evidence. It might consist of other writers' criticisms of a concept or of factual information which contradicts an argument. If you have found evidence of bias or distortion, you need to identify the reasons and justify why you consider the bias to exist. You need to provide accurate references for information. Who said it? When?

What evidence can you provide for your criticisms and evaluation of your topic?

Criticism/evaluation	Evidence

16.7 IMPROVING YOUR SKILLS

Which aspects of gathering information do you need to improve on, and what action could you take to help you improve?

The following will help you plan ahead:

Aspects to be improved	Actions to be taken	By (deadline)

NOTES

NOTES

16.8 REFERENCES AND BIBLIOGRAPHY

Libraries may have materials on this skill area. The following give examples:

Bell, J. (1987), *Doing Your Own Research Project: A Guide for First-time Researchers in Education and Social Science*, Open University Press.

Cohen, L. and Manion, L. (1985 edn), *Research Methods in Education*, Croom Helm.

Deer Richardson, L. (1992), *Techniques of Investigation: An Introduction to Research Methods*, National Extension College.

Huff, D. (1973), *How to Lie with Statistics*, Penguin Books.

Reynolds J. E. F. (ed) (1993), *Martindale the Extra Pharmacopoeia*, The London Pharmaceutical Press.

17
ESSAY WRITING
by Theresa Lillis

CONTENTS

This SkillPack assumes that you are familiar with the basic requirements of an essay. If this is not the case you should consult the equivalent SkillPack in Part I. Here we suggest ways in which an adequate essay can be turned into a good one. This SkillPack focuses on how to explore an essay question critically, how to develop a strong argument and how to critically evaluate different types of evidence.

We suggest you use this SkillPack:

- **before you begin any work on your essay (see Sections 17.1 and 17.2)**
- **once you have first draft, to review and improve it (see Section 17.3 onwards).**

When you have completed it, you should be able to:

1 present the essay in a clearly structured form, appropriate for its purpose and audience
2 produce a sequenced argument, reflected in the structure of the essay
3 plan strategies for producing the essay and criticise those plans
4 act on your understanding of the explicit and implicit tasks in the title and critically review the essay question
5 gather, sort and present evidence to substantiate a case and evaluate that evidence, using appropriate referencing techniques
6 follow standard conventions for grammar, spelling and punctuation
7 use appropriate conventions of academic presentation – eg referencing
8 comply with the regulations on plagiarism
9 critically evaluate the effectiveness of the final draft and identify areas for future improvement
10 seek and use feedback to improve performance.

You should be able to use this skill on your course with little guidance from others.

17.1 A BRIEF REVIEW OF THE BASICS

The equivalent SkillPack in Part I covers the basic requirements for producing an essay. We suggest you use the following to check that you are able to meet those requirements.

	Do you need to improve on this?		Action to be taken
	Yes	No	
Finding out what is expected.			
Gathering information.			
Expressing your ideas clearly.			
Organising points into a meaningful sequence.			
Supporting your argument.			
Referencing.			
Revising your drafts.			
Editing your drafts.			
Producing a clear structure.			
Presenting the essay appropriately.			
Using feedback from your tutors.			

If you feel you could improve on any of the above, the following could help:

- **The equivalent SkillPack in Part I**
- **Examples of essays from your subject area (your lecturer may be able to help)**
- **The chapters on "Gathering and Using Information" (see Contents).**

17.2 CRITICALLY REVIEWING THE ESSAY QUESTION

In order to write a good essay you need to respond both to the explicit (what is obviously stated) and implicit (what is not clearly stated) demands of the question (see the equivalent SkillPack in Part I, Section 6.3).

As you become more confident, you should also explore the underlying assumptions of the essay question. We suggest that you look at these examples and then analyse the underlying assumptions in your own essay question:

Essay question	Underlying assumptions	Questions that should be raised in the essay
Discuss the problems caused by private car use in the city centre and the potential advantages of using alternative means of transport.	• that there are problems caused by private car use	• What problems are caused? • Could these problems be solved?
	• that it would be better to use other forms of transport	• What other forms of transport?
	• that other forms of transport have specific advantages	• What are the advantages of other forms of transport?
	• that there are no other problems caused by alternative forms of transport	• Are there any problems associated with other forms of transport?

Essay question	Underlying assumptions	Questions that should be raised in the essay
Analyse the relationship between educational achievement and ethnic background.	• that "ethnic background" is a meaningful concept	• What does "ethnic background" mean?
	• that educational achievement is a meaningful concept	• What is meant by "educational achievement"?
	• that there is a relationship.	• Is it possible to relate ethnic background to educational achievement?

NOTES	Essay question	Underlying assumptions	Questions that should be raised in your essay
	Your essay title:		
	Your essay title:		

17.3 DEVELOPING A CONVINCING ARGUMENT IN YOUR ESSAY

We suggest you use the rest of this SkillPack to review and redraft an essay you are writing. Reviewing and amending drafts is an essential part of good writing. This section identifies what makes a strong argument in an essay and suggests how you might improve the argument of your current essay. We suggest you do this by firstly thinking about how to sequence your ideas in your essay in general, and secondly, by examining your ideas at paragraph level.

17.3.1 Evaluating argument: focus on sequencing

Although there is no one way of linking paragraphs you must organise them into a meaningful sequence. You construct an argument – a clearly expressed line of thought – by linking ideas across paragraphs.

Examples 1 and 2 show how the argument is often presented in student essays. There are shortcomings in both. Example 3 provides a third alternative to illustrate what a successfully presented argument might look like. The essay question used is:

Discuss the problems caused by private car use in the city centre and the potential advantages of using alternative means of transport.

Example 1 – where the writer's main concern is to include relevant information:

Gives Information
Details about the number of cars used in the city centre at different times of the day.

Gives Information
Details about the pollutants being emitted from cars

Gives Information
Details about the rising incidence of asthma and bronchitis.

Gives Information
Details about all the alternative forms of transport that could be used.

Comment

In this example the writer presents much relevant information but in point form. Each paragraph stands alone, and there is no attempt to explicitly link them in order to give a clear shape to the argument.

Example 2 - where the writer's main concern is to present a straightforward argument against the use of cars:

Introduction
States that the essay will focus on the problems caused by use of large numbers of cars and the advantages of alternative means of transport
Makes claim
High number of cars used causes many problems, notably environmental pollution and risk of accident and injury
Gives information
Details about rising incidence of asthma and bronchitis
Makes claim
Greater use of public transport would significantly reduce risks to health
Concluding comments
Need to develop strategies to encourage greater use of public transport.

Comment

The writer attempts to structure the argument by: stating the focus of the essay, making claims about the disadvantages of car use and the advantages of public transport, making brief concluding comments. However, there is no explicit link made between the main sections. The conclusion is an extension of the list of points made rather than a summary of the argument.

Example 3 – where the writer explicitly links sections in order to present a clearly shaped argument

Please note that this example is a suggestion. There is **no one correct structure** for an essay.

Line of argument	What the writer does
Introduction	
The essay will examine: • the type of problem caused by car use in the city centre • the potential advantages of alternative means of transport. The conclusion will point to the need for policies at local and national levels in order to effect change.	States what will be explored in order to come to some understanding of the key issues.

Main body of essay

NOTES

Section 1

- gives details of personal car use in the city centre
- states the problems, highlighting impact on health and environment
- questions the effectiveness of car use, given that heavy congestion means reaching destination later.

Uses evidence to show high number of cars, increasing incidence of asthma in young children, scientific reports on greenhouse effect.

Focuses on the principal problems caused by personal car use in the city centre.

Linking statement

eg "In the next section, I will suggest ways in which alternative means of transport would help to alleviate some of these problems."

Links Sections 1 and 2 by saying will consider how problems mentioned in Section 1 could be resolved.

Section 2

- gives details of alternative forms of transport for travelling to the city, public and private
- points to the potential for reducing risk to the environment, health.

Uses evidence to show small-scale projects already exist in England, alternative models from other countries, and uses statistical information to show how pollution can be reduced.

Discusses alternative means of transport. Highlights the advantages.

Linking statement

eg "However, whilst there are considerable advantages in using alternative forms of transport relating to health and the environment, there are also disadvantages which deserve consideration."

Links Sections 2 and 3 by saying that there is a need to consider problem areas.

Section 3

- discusses disadvantages of alternative transport for certain sections of population – eg access for elderly and disabled, safety for women travelling at night
- suggests possible solutions to above problems – eg cheap taxi fares for certain groups, more bus routes and buses, taking people closer to home

Discusses potential disadvantages of using alternative forms of transport and suggests ways of dealing with them.

NOTES

- highlights need for policies at local and national levels if wide-ranging changes are to be implemented.

Uses evidence to show concerns of certain groups about alternative forms of transport, points to practices already existing – eg late night minibus services for women travelling alone.

Conclusion

Summarises points made. Highlights implications:

- Clearly there are problems caused by increasing personal car use which are having a serious impact on our health and environment.
- Such problems could be alleviated by use of alternative forms of transport.
- Enforced car use reduction would cause difficulties for certain sections of the population, but a series of measures could be introduced to ensure access and safety.
- Radical changes require careful planning, thus a need for coordinated policy-making and implementation at local and national level.

Summarises points made and highlights practical implications of position taken in essay.

Look at the first draft of your essay. Make a summary list of the points in each paragraph. Are they in the best order? What are the links? Using the framework below try to re-order your points highlighting the links you will make between sections. You may wish to take several copies of this sheet, as you may have more than two paragraphs in the main part of your essay.

Your essay title:

Line of argument
Introduction
Linking statement
Main part of essay: Paragraph 1
Linking statement
Paragraph 2
Linking statement
Conclusion

NOTES

17.3.2 Evaluating argument: focusing on paragraphs

Paragraphs are important building blocks in constructing an argument. Within the paragraphs we suggest you need to do three things: make claims; provide evidence for your claims; question key aspects.

1 **Claims.** Do you make claims about the subject matter in relation to the question?

2 **Information or evidence.** Do you present information simply because it has relevance to the whole subject area or do you present evidence to support the claims made?

3 **Questioning.** Do you question key aspects relating to the essay question – ie underlying assumptions (see section 17.2), or are key terms and concepts taken for granted?

Try to analyse what is going on in each of the paragraphs in the following drafts focusing on **claims**; **evidence** or **information**; **questioning**.

Identifying possible strengths and weaknesses in the examples should help you identify what makes a good argument and hence help you to improve your own essay draft.

Paragraph 1

Alternative means of transport such as buses, trams and bicycles should be used in the city. Some 200 000 cars cross the city centre every day. This means that approximately 250 000 people – 50 per cent of the population – travel by car each day. Such heavy use of private cars causes congestion in the city centre which leads to chemical and noise pollution. The public car parks are saturated, causing even more congestion as drivers look for places to park. Public opinion seems to be that we should reduce the number of cars going into the city centre, but this seems unlikely given the large number of people who choose to travel by car.

Paragraph 2

Alternative forms of transport can be grouped under two headings: public and private. Public transport, such as buses, trains and trams is already in use as a means of travelling into the city centre with some 300 000 people using the main bus company alone. Private transport, such as motorbike and pedal bikes, which emit little or no toxic fumes, are also currently used, although the dangers faced by cyclists on the roads have recently been highlighted. In areas of the city where traffic management schemes have been in operation, pollutants have been reduced by 20 per cent. However, although it is assumed that greater use of public transport such as buses will contribute to reducing pollution, given the state of the old and worn engines, this is unlikely.

17.3.3 Identifying strengths and weaknesses at paragraph level in your essay

Now try to identify the strengths and weaknesses in the two paragraph examples above and then in your own current essay draft.

✔

Tick if:	Paragraph 1	Paragraph 2	Your current draft
all the claims are relevant to the question			
all the claims follow the line of thought/argument			
evidence is provided to support the claims			
key aspects relating to the essay title are questioned			
evidence is provided to illustrate questions raised			
all information provided is relevant to the argument in the essay			

17.3.4 Evaluating the argument in your own writing

✍

Are you satisfied that your essay...	Yes	No	Revisions to be made
has an overall structure which: • answers the question? • has a clear introduction and main body which has an argument running through? • presents relevant information?			
has a conclusion which: • is relevant? • summarises the argument? • follows logically from the argument? • shows the implications of the argument?			

NOTES

Are you satisfied that your essay...	Yes	No	Revisions to be made
at paragraph level: • makes claims relevant to the question? • makes claims which are central to the overall argument? • presents information as part of evidence • critically evaluates evidence? • questions and explores key aspects?			

signposts the sequence of argument by:
• highlighting main points by use of language?
• being concise?
• reminding readers:
    – what your argument is?
    – what the argument is at different points in your essay?
    – where your argument is going?			

17.4 CRITICALLY EVALUATING THE EVIDENCE

You are often asked to be critical in your writing. This means that:

• **you must not accept ideas, information, opinions and research findings at face value**
• **you must question underlying attitudes, approaches and assumptions and discuss them in your essay.**

You could ask yourself...	How will this affect your argument?
What are my own views on this issue?	
What would the opposite views be?	
Whose side am I on in this issue?	

You could ask yourself...	How will this affect your argument?
Are any values or political issues involved?	
Would I like the reader to come to any particular conclusions?	

NOTES

17.4.2 Others' assumptions

What are your sources of information	How might they be biased	How will you use this source in your argument?

NOTES

17.4.3 Balanced information

Information might be distorted either intentionally or unintentionally. Can you identify balance and the reasons for it? For example:

- **highlighting an individual case and generalising from it**
- **personalising/anecdotes**
- **graphs or diagrams not to scale**
- **dubious causal relationships.**

Questions you might ask include:

- **What is the sample on which any generalisation is based?** A generalisation based on a sample of two may be less valid than a generalisation based on a sample of 2000.
- **Are there any other possible interpretations of this information?**
- **Is it accurate?**
- **What question was asked?** For example:

Interviewer: "Which political party do you support?"

Respondent: "Conservative"

Interviewer: "Do you vote in elections?"

Respondent: "No"

If only the first question was used to gauge electoral support the results might be very misleading.

17.4.4 Presenting your criticisms and evaluation of the information

It is important to make any criticisms clear for the reader. In criticisms and evaluation of information it helps to do the following:

- **Back up criticisms and evaluation with evidence.**
- **Make your own biases, assumptions and stance clear.**
- **Make any biases, assumptions or stances by others clear** – eg *"X states that ..."*, *"Y states that ..."*, *"X appears to assume that ... Y, on the other hand, assumes ..."*.
- **Be concise.** Long-winded explanations are tedious.
- **Be relevant.** Are your criticisms and evaluation relevant to your purpose or are you going off at a tangent?
- **Be meaningful to the reader.** What might seem crucial to one reader may seem trivial to another.

17.5 SIGNPOSTING TO MAKE YOUR ARGUMENT EXPLICIT

NOTES

A common problem in essays is that the argument is not clearly enough stated. Signposting your points can help to make your argument explicit. You can do this by:

- **clear headings** (where recommended to be used)
- **clear section numbering** (where recommended to be used)
- **use of images/visuals where appropriate**
- **a logical order**
- **being concise**
  - removing padding
  - removing repetition
  - removing too much detail
- **telling the reader what s/he has just read** *("To summarise …")*
- **telling the reader what is coming next** *("As the following section indicates …").*

17.5.1 Using language to signpost the direction of your argument

To point towards the conclusion:

............so...
............thus...
............therefore....................................
............hence..
............we can conclude that.........................
............consequently.................................

To show how claims and evidence lead to a certain conclusion:

............shows that...................................
............indicates that...............................
............proves that..................................
............entails that.................................
............implies that.................................
............establishes that.............................
............allows us to infer that......................
............gives us reason for believing that.....

To show how the conclusions are the result of claims and evidence:

............is shown by..................................
............is indicated by..............................
............is proven by ....
............is implied by................................
............is established by............................
............is entailed by...............................

Based on Cederblom and Paulsen (1990)

NOTES

17.6 USING FEEDBACK ON YOUR ESSAY

The most common form of feedback from tutors is by means of written comments on your essay. Many tutors will also discuss their comments with you. Feedback is useful as it helps to explain why you have been given a particular grade, and it can be used to improve future essays.

When you get feedback from your tutor:

- **Read or listen to the comments carefully.**
- **Check that you understand the points being made. If you aren't sure, ask.**
- **Discuss with your tutor areas on which to concentrate when writing your next essay.**
- **Categorise the comments made.** For example, are there many comments on your referencing techniques or on the development of your argument? Compare the comments made with previous comments to see if there are particular areas you need to work on.
- **Compare the feedback from your tutor with your own assessment of your essay to identify points for further discussion.**
- **Reread your feedback and any notes you make before completing your next essay.**

17.7 IDENTIFYING USEFUL STRATEGIES FOR FUTURE WRITING

Writing an essay involves a range of activities, some of which are highlighted in the diagram below.

Try to make notes in the relevant boxes of the strategies you found useful in writing your current essay and which you might use again. For example, you may have found it helpful to ask a friend to read a draft to see if s/he could follow your argument.

Analysing a question

It was helpful to:

Gathering information

It was helpful to:

Generating ideas

It was helpful to:

Constructing an argument

It was helpful to:

Critically evaluating information

It was helpful to:

Drafting ideas

It was helpful to:

Leading the reader to the conclusion

It was helpful to:

NOTES

17.8 REFERENCES AND FURTHER READING

Libraries may have material on this skill area. The following give examples:

Brown, S., Rust, C. and Gibbs, G. (1994), *Strategies for Diversifying Assessment*, Oxford Centre for Staff Development.

Cederblom, J. and Paulsen, P. W. (1990), *Critical Reasoning*, (3rd edn), Wadsworth.

Further reading

Clancy, J. and Ballard, B. (1992), *How to Write Essays: A Practical Guide for Students*, Longman.
(Good general overview.)

Fairbairn, G. J. and Winch, C. (1991), *Reading, Writing and Reasoning: A Guide for Students*, Society for Research into Higher Education and Oxford University Press.
(See Chapter 2 for problems facing students when writing. See Chapter 3 for discussion and examples of different types of reasoning used in writing.)

Newby, M. (1989), *Writing. A Guide for Students*, Cambridge University Press.
(See Chapter 2 for details on punctuation, sentence structure, paragraphing.)

18
REPORT WRITING

by Sue Drew and Rosie Bingham

CONTENTS

The report is a common way of presenting information and advice related to a specific purpose. It is used by industry, business, commerce, professional bodies, charities and government as a basis for decisions and policies. University and college courses aim to develop this skill in students because it will be applicable in all professional contexts. Employers want graduates and higher diplomates who can write effective reports.

This SkillPack aims to help you turn an adequate report into a good one, and produce more in-depth and professional reports, as you would at work.

We suggest you use this SkillPack:

- **in conjunction with a report you need to write**
- **before you begin any work**
- **while you are gathering information and writing your report.**

When you have completed it, you should be able to:

1 identify the purpose of the report and the needs and characteristics of the audience
2 include accurate information appropriate to the purpose and audience, and criticise and evaluate the information, identifying reasons for any bias or distortion
3 decide on, and use, a format appropriate to the subject area, purpose and audience, and present it legibly and with a clear layout
4 use images to support or clarify main points
5 use language which is appropriate for the subject area, purpose and the audience and use grammar, punctuation and spelling which follow standard conventions
6 clearly signpost for the audience the critical points or issues
7 evaluate the effectiveness of the report for the purpose and the audience and identify areas for future improvement.

You should be able to use these elements of the skill in your course and in your professional practice (eg placements), with little or no support from tutors, lecturers or others.

18.1 A BRIEF REVIEW OF THE BASICS

The equivalent SkillPack in Part I covers the basic requirements for producing a report.

Can you meet these requirements?

	Yes	Some-what	No
Are you clear about the purpose of your report?			
Have you identified your readers' needs and characteristics?			
Have you identified what needs to be done and planned your time?			
Have you allowed time to draft, write, edit and present your report?			
Do you know the information needed and how to gather it?			
Can you use the information accurately?			
Do you need permission to use the material – eg from the author, employer or other source?			
Do you know the correct format of a report for your subject?			
Can you order information and identify the main points?			
Can you present a report clearly and attractively?			
Do you know when to use images or visuals?			
Is your language appropriate for the subject, purpose, readers?			
Do you edit your draft?			

If you feel you could improve on any of the above the following can help:

• **the equivalent SkillPack in Part I**
• **examples of reports from your subject area (consult libraries or your lecturer)**
• **the chapters on "Gathering and Using Information" (see Contents)**
• **the chapters on "Organising Yourself and Your Time" (see Contents).**

18.2 GETTING INSIDE YOUR READER'S HEAD

NOTES

Good reports meet the reader's needs. You may be asked to produce a report for other students, for your lecturers, or perhaps for outside organisations or workplace supervisors. What will your reader need and why? It can help to put yourself in her/his position.

If I were the reader...
Why would I want the report?
What would I want it to tell me?
What sort of language would I understand?
What sort of language would impress or persuade me?
What aspects might I find difficult to understand?

NOTES

18.3 CRITICISING AND EVALUATING THE INFORMATION

A good report gives accurate and objective information. It should also criticise and evaluate the information. Being critical and evaluative means not accepting information at face value but asking why it is as it is.

18.3.1 Your own assumptions

Are there any possible reasons for bias in yourself?

You could ask yourself...
What are my own views on the issue?
What would the opposite views be?
Do I have an existing stance before I start my investigations?
Whose side am I on concerning this issue?
Are any values or political issues involved?
Would I like the reader to come to any particular conclusions?

You can continually refer back to these notes and ask the following questions when looking at your information.

- **Am I presenting this objectively?**
- **How would somebody with opposing views present this information?**

18.3.2 Others' assumptions

Might the sources of your information be biased? For example, the tobacco industry may have a vested interest in downgrading the risks of smoking; non-smokers, who dislike others' smoke, may have a vested interest in highlighting the risks of smoking.

What are your sources of information?	How might they be biased?

NOTES

18.3.3 Distorted information

Information might be distorted intentionally or unintentionally. Can you identify distortion and the reasons for it?

Possible distortion	Example/possible queries
Highlighting an individual case and generalising from it	eg Child abduction. Very few children are abducted but a publicised case causes general anxiety.
Personalising/anecdotes	eg *"All the trains I use are late"*. How often do you go on a train? Is it always the same route, or time, or day? What are the actual figures?
Graphs or diagrams not to scale	eg See Huff (1973) for examples of how to lie with statistics.
Dubious causal relationships	eg Do men achieve higher scores than women in a spatial ability test because they have a higher ability or because the test questions relate to male interests?

Questions you might ask should include:

- **What is the sample on which a generalisation is based? If it is based on a sample of two it may be less valid than if based on a sample of 2000.**
- **Are there any other possible interpretations of this information?**
- **Is it accurate?**
- **What question was asked?**
  - eg **Interviewer** "Which political party do you support?"
    Respondent "Conservative"
    Interviewer "Do you vote in elections?"
    Respondent "No".

If only the first question was used to gauge electoral support the results might be very misleading.

Use the box below to identify any distorted information in your report.

Possible distortion	Example/possible queries

18.3.4 Presenting your criticisms and evaluation of the information

Good reports make any criticisms clear for the reader. It helps to:

- **back up criticisms and evaluation with evidence**
- **make your own biases, assumptions and stance clear**
- **make any biases, assumptions or stances by others clear** – eg *" X states that...."*, *" Y states that..."*, *"X appears to assume that... Y, on the other hand, assumes..."*
- **be concise** – long-winded explanations are tedious
- **be relevant** – make sure your criticisms and evaluation are relevant to your purpose and that you are not going off at a tangent
- **be meaningful to the reader** – what might seem crucial to one reader may seem trivial to another.

Information	Criticism	Evidence

NOTES

18.4 SIGNPOSTING

A reader should very quickly be able to extract the relevant information. Busy readers will want to scan the report to see what is relevant to them and then to read certain sections in more detail.

Help the reader to do this by:

- **stimulating interest**
- **highlighting crucial points**
- **clear "signposting".**

18.4.1 Main points

Start by being clear about the crucial points which you must convey to the reader. List these below:

Crucial points

Then ask yourself:

- **What will interest readers?**
- **What angle is most likely to capture their interest?**
- **What do I want them to be most interested in?**

The answers to these questions can influence how you order your material. There is little point in having a fascinating conclusion if the reader has stopped reading long ago. Use your introduction to gain interest.

18.4.2 Signposting

Signposting means helping the reader find their way through your report. The following are possibilities:

- a **contents page**
- an **introduction** which explains what is to follow, or an initial **summary** or **synopsis** of the main points
- clear **headings**
- clear **section numbering**
- a **logical order**
- a clear **layout** – use of bullets, short blocks of text
- use of **images/visuals** at appropriate points (some information makes more impact, and is more understandable if presented visually)
- being **concise** – removing padding, repetition and too much detail
- **summarising** – telling the reader what s/he has just read (*"to summarise ..."*)
- **leading** – telling the reader what is coming next (*"as the following section indicates ..."*).

18.5 IMPROVING THE EFFECTIVENESS OF YOUR REPORTS

How effective is your report and what do you need to do to improve in the future? It will help in completing the exercise below if you look at your report as the reader would. It will be even more useful if you can get feedback from your readers.

	Notes on improvement needed	Actions to be taken
Identifying purposes		
Identifying readers' needs		
Time planning		
Format of the report		
Information-gathering		
Presentation		
Images/visuals		
Criticising/ evaluating		
Signposting		

18.6 REFERENCES AND BIBLIOGRAPHY

Libraries may have materials on this skill area. The following give examples:

Bell, J. (1987), *Doing your Research Project: A Guide for First-time Researchers in Education and Social Science*, Open University Press.

Cooper, B. M. (1964), *Writing Technical Reports*, Penguin Books.

Gowers, E. (1986), *The Complete Plain Words*, HMSO.

Huff, D. (1973), *How to Lie with Statistics*, Penguin Books.

Peel, M. (1990), *Improving Your Communication Skills*, Kogan Page.

Stanton, N. (1990), *Communication*, Macmillan Education.

19
ORAL PRESENTATION

by Sue Drew and Rosie Bingham

CONTENTS

The verbal skills which are critical in oral presentations are much in demand by employers, who see communication skills as vital. In order to develop these skills many courses require students to make oral presentations – providing inputs for seminars or tutorials, or making individual or group presentations on projects.

Oral presentations can be useful in assessment as they demonstrate abilities in a way which does not require written skills, and they allow for dialogue (a viva is an example of an oral exam).

We suggest you use this SkillPack:

- **to help you prepare for an actual presentation**
- **to refer to before you begin any preparatory work.**

When you have completed it, you should be able to:

1 select material which is appropriate for the purpose and the audience
2 structure material for the purpose and the audience
3 prepare relevant visual aids which clearly illustrate points (eg legible OHP slides)
4 present visual aids effectively and at appropriate junctures
5 use language, tone and manner (including non verbal behaviour) suited to the purpose and audience, and which draw on your personal style
6 encourage audience participation (eg questions) and respond effectively
7 actively check audience understanding, observe audience reaction and make appropriate responses
8 for group presentations, allocate tasks which make best use of individual abilities and expertise.

You should be able to use the above elements of the skill on your course, on work placement or in your professional practice, with little or no support.

19.1 INTRODUCTION

19.1.1 Your existing skills

The equivalent SkillPack in Part I covered the essentials. These are listed below and you can rate yourself against each item, where 1 = "very good" and 4 = "in need of considerable attention". If your rating indicates that you need to give attention to any items you should refer back to the equivalent SkillPack in Part I.

✔

Existing skills	1	2	3	4
Identifying aims and objectives for the presentation.				
Identifying audience characteristics and needs.				
Identifying the time available.				
Checking out the room/location, its facilities and seating.				
Selecting material to use.				
Structuring material.				
Having useful speaker's notes.				
Preparing and using visual aids.				
Preparing the delivery: • being well organised • your voice and manner • dealing with questions.				
Combating nerves.				

19.1.2 What makes a presentation good?

If you can do all the above your presentation should be satisfactory, but you could make it better. What makes a presentation really good? It may help to think of individuals you know (a teacher, lecturer, other students, salesperson, politician) and identify what makes them good or bad. Does the situation in which the presentation takes place influence what is appropriate?

Presenter	What they do

NOTES

19.2 USING YOUR PERSONAL STYLE

19.2.1 Strengths and weaknesses

It is important to know and play to your strengths and to identify your weaknesses and allow for them. If you are a terrible joke teller it may be better to avoid jokes; if you are very good at visuals, you could emphasise visual aids. Once you have identified your strengths and weaknesses, you must decide what to do about them.

For example:

Strengths	Weaknesses
funny	*nervous*
strong voice	*fidgeting*
open manner	*too quiet*
good sense of timing	*rambling/over wordy*
concise/pithy	*unfocused*
relaxed	*aggressive*
provocative	*defensive*

What are yours? If necessary, refer back to Section 19.1.2 for help.

Strengths	Weaknesses

NOTES

How can you allow for weaknesses?

If you find it difficult to think of solutions to your particular problems, you could ask friends or tutors for ideas.

Possibilities are:

- **Fidgeting.** Find something constructive to do with your hands (eg put OHP slides on, hold prompt cards).
- **Quiet voice.** Use lots of visual aids, rearrange the seating, use a microphone if you have a large audience.
- **Nervous.** Use visual aids to direct attention away from you and on to the visuals; wear something to give you confidence; be well prepared; sit/stand in a comfortable position.

How can you maximise your strengths?

- **Humour.** Devise a way of fitting your particular brand of humour into the presentation.
- **Good sense of timing.** Consider incorporating different types of short inputs.
- **Provocative.** Give the audience a chance to react to your statements and space to challenge or argue.

Actions I can take

19.3 USING GROUP MEMBERS IN GROUP PRESENTATIONS

If you are giving a group presentation, it may help to refer to the chapters on "Group Work" (see Contents). How can you use all the group members in the presentation, and how can you use their particular skills and minimise their weaknesses?

When allocating roles, consider the following:

- **Who knows more about/has a special interest in a topic?**
- **Who could attract the audience's attention at the start?**
- **Who is good at explaining detail?**
- **Who is good at using projectors, videos, models?**
- **Who is good at fielding questions?**
- **Who can put forward a point of view strongly?**
- **Who can appear sympathetic or open and encourage the audience to speak?**

You may want to try something you are not very good at (if you don't try you never will be). You can also check with group members what they'd like to try and, if they are nervous about it, offer ideas, help and support.

Group member	Task/role in the presentation

19.4 AUDIENCE PARTICIPATION

19.4.1 Getting audience reaction

Good presenters engage with the audience. Again you might refer back to your observations in Section 19.1.2. How do good presenters do this?

Use the following checklist to assess your skills and also add any other items you can think of. Which skills or behaviours do you use now and which could you try to do more frequently?

✔

Audience engagement skills/behaviours	Use now	Could use more
Maintain eye contact (not with one person, but scanning the audience).		
Ask if they can hear you or see the visual aids.		
Check they are comfortable. Do the windows need opening/shutting?		
Make references to them and their interests or needs.		
Ask if they have understood.		
Ask for questions.		
Ask if anybody has different or additional views or information.		
Watch for signs of boredom or restlessness (looking at watches/out of windows/yawning/dropped heads and slumped shoulders/putting coats on).		
Watch for signs of irritation (body language such as sitting on the edge of seats, facial expressions).		
Watch for those who want to speak (hands up, sitting forward, mouths open, interruptions).		

NOTES

19.4.2 Responding to audience reactions

How do you respond to an audience's reaction to your presentation? Part of the answer to this depends on your personal style.

You should respond in a way with which you are comfortable but you also need to be able to handle the consequences.

The following chart suggests possible responses:

Possible response	Advantages	Disadvantages
Response with humour	*Releases tension*	*The audience may feel put down*
Response with a challenge	*Generates discussion*	*May lead to an argument*
Calming response	*Reduces tension*	*The audience may feel patronised*
A straight answer	*Creates trust and openness*	*Probably won't cause difficulties*

Other possible responses may not depend on your personal style.

For example, if people are bored or restless:

- **move on to another section**
- **use a visual aid**
- **ask them a question or for an opinion**
- **finish quickly.**

If people look irritated:

- **ask for their opinions and deal with the irritation.**

When you give your presentation you could ask yourself afterwards how you responded, what worked and what you would do differently in future (see the assessment box on the next page).

Audience reaction	My response	What I'd do in future

NOTES

19.4.3 Responding to questions

If you encourage audience participation you are likely to generate questions or comments. How can you deal with them? Politely. Putting somebody down will discourage others from speaking. What are other possible responses and their consequences?

Response	Possible effect
A straight reply	*Welcomed*
"I'm afraid I don't know, does anybody else?"	*Welcomed*
Waffle	*Irritation, lack of respect*
"What do you think?" (back to the questioner)	*Either flattered or put on the spot*
"I wonder if Jane can answer that?"	*OK if Jane knows the answer. If not, she may be annoyed*
Answer a different question	*Irritation*

What are your concerns in dealing with questions? What could you do about it?

Concerns	Possible actions

19.4.4 Timing

It is much easier to keep to time with no audience participation – you just practise the presentation in advance and time it. But good presentations involve the audience.

How much audience participation do you want? Allowing 10 minutes for questions or discussion at the end is easy to plan for. However, if you want to involve the audience throughout, possibilities are:

- **Reduce your material (eg to two-thirds or half of what you could cover with no participation).**
- **Have extra material available in case the audience keeps quiet.**
- **Be tough on timing. Allow a specific time for each section and move on** *(eg "I'm afraid we need to move on if we are going to cover everything"; "Can we stop at that point and move on?").*

Do not overrun! Your audience may have other things to do or the room may be needed by another group.

19.5 COMBATING NERVES

If you use the equivalent SkillPack in Part I to get the essentials right, this should help a great deal. Being prepared, well organised and having good visual aids are very important in dealing with nerves. You could also look at the chapters on "Coping with Pressure" (see Contents).

What might make you nervous? What happens when you are nervous? What could you do about this? It might help to look back over this SkillPack and ask which of the ideas you have gained:

a) you could feel comfortable with
b) would stretch you a bit
c) would scare you.

Why not include in your presentation a lot of (a), some of (b) and little of (c)? Practice does much to reduce nerves. Next time you will find some of the things you thought would stretch you are now OK, and some of those which seemed scarey fall into the "stretching" category.

Why not watch other presentations or videos to become more familiar with techniques? Ask others how they deal with nerves. You may be surprised at how even those who appear most confident also suffer from nerves.

19.6 REVIEWING YOUR PERFORMANCE

A way to improve your skills is to think through what you did afterwards, and ask for feedback from your audience. You could do this verbally, one-to-one, or you could hand out an evaluation form seeking feedback on areas to which you want to give attention. After your presentation the following checklist could help you to identify actions needed for the next one:

Preparation

Using your personal style

Getting audience reaction

Responding to audience reaction

Responding to questions

Timing

Combating nerves

19.7 REFERENCES AND BIBLIOGRAPHY

Libraries may have materials on this skill area. The following give examples:

Bernstein, D. (1988), *Put It Together. Put It Across. The Craft of Business Presentation*, Cassell.

Peel, M. (1990), *Improving your Communication Skills*, Kogan Page.

Peel, M. (1992), *Successful Presentation in a Week*, Hodder & Stoughton.

Stanton, N. (1990), *Communication*, Macmillan Education.

Videos

The Floor is Yours Now – A Guide to Successful Presentations, Gower (24 minutes).

We Can't Hear You at The Back, (part of a series – *Work is a Four-letter Word*) BBC 1992 (30 minutes).

Laser Disc

Discovering Presentations, (interactive video) Longmans Training: British Telecom 1991.

NOTES

20 SOLVING PROBLEMS

by Sue Drew and Rosie Bingham

CONTENTS

Many of the assignments or activities you have to undertake on a course are concerned with solving problems – eg projects, case studies, essays, seminar discussions, examinations. The reason for this is that employers rate problem-solving ability very highly, and lecturers want students to develop their skills in this area.

Graduates and higher diplomates are expected to solve unanticipated problems at work, and to be capable of more than merely carrying out routine procedures.

We suggest you use this SkillPack:

- **when you have an assignment, course or placement activity which involves solving problems**
- **before you begin work on the assignment or task**
- **then whilst you are working on it.**

When you have completed it, you should be able to:

1 collect information and regularly review it to identify where more is needed to clarify critical features and to identify possible solutions
2 select relevant information, investigate contradictory information and identify reasons for it
3 identify critical features of problems which include a broad range of factors and a range of possible solutions and where there is a significant amount of contradictory information
4 where appropriate accurately follow set procedures to clarify. the problem, seek information and identify solutions
5 identify and select efficient and effective procedures to clarify the problem, seek information and identify solutions. Identify general rules to help clarify the problem or select solutions
6 identify and use criteria to select an effective solutions (eg short-term and long-term benefits).

You should be able to use the above elements of the skill on your course, and in your personal life and professional practice (eg placement), with little or no support from tutors, lecturers and others.

20.1 HOW DO YOU CURRENTLY SOLVE PROBLEMS?

Which of the following techniques do you use? If you are unsure about any of them refer to the equivalent SkillPack in Part I (see Contents).

✔

By a logical step-by-step process determined by yourself.	
By following procedures set by somebody else – eg in a lab.	
By trial and error.	
By creative idea generation – eg brainstorming.	
By constructive analysis (identifying advantages, disadvantages, interesting aspects).	
By other means (list):	

How would you rate your ability in the following, using a rating scale where 1 = "very good" and 4 = "in need of considerable improvement"? This SkillPack focuses on these areas.

✔

	1	2	3	4
Identifying the essential elements of a problem.				
Collecting and selecting information to help solve the problem.				
Identifying and using procedures to solve the problem.				
Identifying solutions.				
Deciding on solutions.				
Evaluating solutions.				

How effective are you in solving problems? Add your own items.

✔

I could solve problems in less time (be more efficient).	
I could find better solutions (be more effective).	
I could feel less anxious or enjoy solving problems more.	
Others (please add):	

20.2 PROBLEM-SOLVING PROCESSES

There is no right or wrong way to solve a problem – only a way which is best for the situation and you. You may start by:

- **generating possible solutions**

or

- **identifying what procedures you will use**

or

- **identifying the essential elements of a problem.**

Whatever your starting point, at some stage you need to give attention to the following aspects. We have presented this in a circle rather than in linear form, since it is important to acknowledge that there is no single right way.

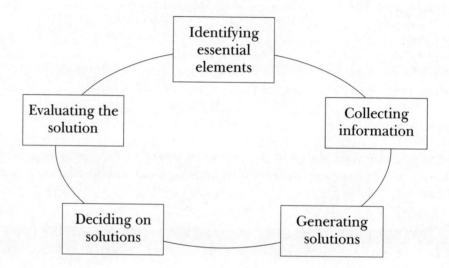

20.3 COLLECTING EVIDENCE

20.3.1 What do you want to know?

What do you need to know about your problem? For example:

- **What have you been asked to do?**
- **Who for?**
- **Why?**
- **By when?**
- **What are the constraints (what might limit your solutions)?**
- **What is the context (what situational factors must you take into account)?**
- **Is this problem similar to others you have encountered? What aspects are similar?**

The questions may differ according to the problem. What do you need to know before you solve your problem?

Questions I need to answer about my problem

20.3.2 Contradictory information

It can help to identify what information is contradictory. For example:

- **a seminar discussion** – eg one person is entertaining and interesting **but** talks too much and prevents others from talking
- **a project about energy** – eg the cheapest fuel is also the most environmentally damaging
- **work** – eg you need a part-time job to earn money **but** it will take time from studying.

What are the contradictory aspects of **your** problem? Why are they contradictory? Resolving these contradictions may be crucial to the problem-solving process.

Contradictory elements	Why are they contradictory?

20.3.3 Reviewing your information

You may need to continue to gather information to clarify the problem. One of these pieces of information may lead to a new question or angle. For example:

- **Project about energy.** Can coal emissions from power stations be reduced? What will it cost? What is the cost in relation to, say, nuclear power?
- **Part-time job.** What hours must you work? Will they clash with study time? How do you spend the rest of your time?

The following suggests three stages to the information review, but there could be more.

Initial questions	Information/answers

Secondary questions	Information/answers

Final questions	Information/answers

20.3.4 How do you know that you have enough information?

Is it repeating itself?	
Is it adding anything?	
Is it really relevant?	
Will it make a big difference?	
Is it worth the time taken to gather it?	

NOTES

20.4 IDENTIFYING THE ESSENTIAL ELEMENTS OF A PROBLEM

You might ask yourself the following questions in relation to your problem:

What makes it a problem?

What does the solution have to achieve?

Who will need to use/apply the solution? Who is involved?

Are there any practicalities to attend to – eg cost, time, facilities?

Who has vested interests in it?

Others (please add):

You also need to weigh up contradictory information. There are several possible strategies:

- **Identify the advantages and disadvantages of each aspect.**
- **Identify the costs and benefits of each aspect.**
- **Consult others who have an interest in the issue.**
- **Identify your immediate gut reaction/feelings and then question the reaction (eg if somebody told you to take the part-time job, regardless of the course, would you be relieved or worried?).**
- **Gather more information. It might swing the weight of evidence in one direction.**

What other strategies have you or your friends tried?

20.5 GENERATING AND DECIDING ON SOLUTIONS

20.5.1 Generating solutions

The equivalent SkillPack in Part I (see Contents), identifies a range of strategies for generating solutions. They include:

- **brainstorming**
- **trial and error**
- **creative thinking.**

It helps to generate as many ideas for solutions as possible, then to narrow down those you will investigate more seriously, and to do detailed work on the most likely solution. Refer back to the equivalent SkillPack in Part I if you need to.

Remember that focusing from the start on only one solution can limit your ability to solve your problems.

20.5.2 Selecting solutions

General rules or principles

Are there any "general rules" which might help you select solutions, or limit the possible solutions? For example:

- **problems between people.** General rules: people like to be consulted; people like to be listened to.
- **design problem.** General rule: the solution must meet the needs of the user.

General rules to help select a solution

Criteria

What criteria will you use to judge your possible solutions? These will vary from problem to problem and may include both short-term and long-term criteria.

Example: part-time job

Short-term criteria – must:
- *pay £X per week*
- *take up no more than X hours per week*
- *fit in with course timetable*
- *be something I can do.*

Long-term criteria – must:
- *finance me to complete the course*
- *allow me time to do well on the course.*

Criteria against which to judge solutions for my problem

20.6 EVALUATING YOUR EFFECTIVENESS

20.6.1 The problem

Do you have any other, more personal, criteria against which to judge the solution to your problem – eg getting a high mark or grade, reducing the anxiety you feel about solving problems?

20.6.2 Your skills

What are your strengths in solving problems? Where do you need to improve? You could adopt a problem-solving approach to your own skill development. For example:

- **What evidence is there of your problem-solving skills?**
- **What does this reveal about the essential elements of your problem solving?**
- **How could you improve your problem solving?**
- **Which ways of improving your problem solving will you select?**
- **How will you implement them and review their effectiveness?**

You could begin at any point with the above questions and then complete the following:

Areas I need to improve	Action to take

NOTES

NOTES

20.7 REFERENCES AND BIBLIOGRAPHY

Libraries may have materials on this skill. The following give examples:

Comino Foundation (1994), *GRASP® – Getting Results and Solving Problems*, Comino Foundation, 29 Holloway Lane, Amersham, HP6 6DJ

Cowan, J. (nd), *Individual Approaches to Problem Solving*, Department of Civil Engineering, Heriot Watt University.

de Bono, E. (1982), *De Bono's Thinking Course*, Ariel Books, BBC.

21
GROUP WORK
by Sue Drew and Rosie Bingham

CONTENTS

Courses include group work because, in employment, most work is carried out by people working together to share resources, perspectives, ideas and abilities. When recruiting, employers place great store on evidence that you can work well with others.

Group work activities help you develop and practise your own individual skills in working with others, and encourage students to learn from and help each other. While group work can be exciting and enjoyable, a group that is not working well can be frustrating. Improving how you work in groups should improve the end result.

Groups are effective not just because of luck, or because of the particular mix of members, but because of individuals working together to make them effective.

There is no one single "correct" way to behave in a group. This SkillPack aims to help you think about what is happening and to identify strategies which will work for you.

We suggest you use this SkillPack:

- **right at the start of a group activity**
- **and then throughout that activity.**

When you have completed it, you should be able to:

1 clarify, agree and understand group goals; consider and agree relevant basic principles
2 plan action to meet goals and review group and individual progress; review and agree amendments to goals and plans as necessary
3 agree allocation of tasks, taking into account individual skills and knowledge and encouraging flexibility; agree appropriate leadership if needed
4 carry out tasks within agreed limits, using the different perspectives of other group members to improve personal performance
5 contribute to meetings in a way which is relevant, equal and draws on personal skills and knowledge
6 actively seek and listen to the contributions of others
7 request feedback on individual performance (relating to task and behaviour)
8 identify elements of personal performance which are effective or less effective in a range of group situations; plan action to implement appropriate behaviour.

You should be able to use this skill on your course or programme, on work placement or in a professional area, with little or no support from a tutor, working with other students or members of outside organisations.

NOTES

21.1 INTRODUCTION

How do you feel about group work? What are the main issues you want to consider when you work in groups?

Main issues:

eg Will everyone contribute equally?

Will the group work as effectively as an individual?

After you have worked through this SkillPack you can return to this box to check whether your needs have been met.

21.2 CLARIFYING GOALS, SETTING UP THE GROUP

The equivalent SkillPack in Part I suggests that you begin by:

• **agreeing ground rules for how you operate as a group.** This is very important as it sets a positive tone and can avoid future problems.

• **clarifying your goals as a group.** What are you trying to achieve? Do you all have the same understanding of this? Your instructions for your group task may be vague and you may need to agree what you are aiming for.

The Starter level SkillPack mentioned above can refresh your memory on these. Section 21.3 of this Development level SkillPack helps you consider your goals in more detail.

21.3 PLANNING

Consider Sections 21.3.1 and 21.3.2 and then complete Section 21.3.3.

21.3.1 Dividing up tasks

It helps to break your group's task down into sub-tasks with deadlines, which are then allocated to group members. In allocating tasks you could consider:

- **fair and equal workloads**
- **personal interests**
- **members' expertise. Members might want to use their existing expertise or develop new expertise by attempting tasks which are new to them. Group members are a resource and it is important to use them effectively.**

Suppose that you can't agree who will do what. Drawing lots may result in a lack of commitment on the part of some individuals and a failure to do the work. Negotiating is a better method and is an important skill in working with others. The whole group can work together to:

- **identify everybody's preferences**
- **identify conflicts of preferences**
- **identify any solutions – eg redivide or redefine the sub-tasks; work together on a sub-task.**

You may find the chapters on "Negotiating and Assertiveness" helpful (see Contents).

21.3.2 Reviewing goals and plans

Circumstances change. New information comes to light and new angles emerge.

In these cases, you may have to rethink both your goals and the division of sub-tasks and their allocation to individuals. You may also need to extend or develop your project. Progress may produce unexpected issues – you will have to decide, as a group, how to respond to these.

You may need to return to basic principles, review them and agree those you are operating from. These principles might refer to how you operate as a group (eg being honest with each other) or to the task (eg principles relating to your subject such as scientific, engineering or sociological principles; criteria for judging the effectiveness of the product of the group, such as a report).

The following subsection should help you carry out regular reviews – eg at every group meeting.

21.3.3 The plan itself

Initial goals	Amended goals

Initial sub-task	Amended sub-tasks	By (group member)	Deadline

How will you make sure that everybody carries out their agreed tasks? Possibilities include:

- writing down what was agreed
- reviewing progress regularly
- telling the others if you have problems
- trying to help others sort out their problems (this doesn't mean doing the work for them)
- using the chapters on "Negotiating and Assertiveness" (see Contents).

You may need to seek help from your tutor.

21.4 WORKING WITH OTHERS

21.4.1 Using group members

If you work on your sub-task mainly on your own you will miss one of the main benefits of group work – getting ideas, new perspectives and information from others to improve your work. Have you:

- **discussed how you'll go about your sub-task with other group members and checked progress with them?**
- **asked them what information or ideas they have to help you?**
- **discussed how your sub-task relates to theirs?**
- **accepted their views openly and non-defensively?**
- **helped them by discussing their sub-task and reviewing their work?**

21.4.2 Group process

The following may help you think about what is happening in your group. It has a scale of 1-4, where 1 = "very helpful behaviour" and 4 = "very unhelpful behaviour".

In your group do you:	1	2	3	4	
express feelings openly?					grumble afterwards?
ask others for views/ideas?					fail to ask others for their views/ideas?
listen/respond to others?					ignore others/their ideas?
share work evenly?					fail to share work evenly?
participate equally in discussion?					dominate, or keep quiet?
use group members' abilities well?					fail to use group members' abilities well?
help each other?					form cliques/pairs/act uncooperatively?
trust each other?					feel suspicious of each other?
show enthusiasm?					show apathy?
understand group goals?					not understand group goals?
accept group goals?					not accept group goals?
achieve group goals?					fail to achieve group goals?
use resources well?					not use resources well?
all agree decisions?					not make decisions, or fail to involve all?
use time effectively?					not use time effectively?

NOTES

NOTES

What are the reasons for any problems you may have identified by using the above list? For example, if you feel you are wasting time, why does this happen? What could you do differently (eg set deadlines, appoint a "timekeeper" for meetings)? What is **your** part in any problems? What could **you** do personally to improve things? You could return to the group process list at intervals to see if there is any improvement.

The group's main problem	Group action to be taken	Actions to be taken by me

21.4.3 Problems between people

If there are problems between group members (eg somebody not pulling their weight or being domineering), it is important to deal with them, or you may end up with too much work, become resentful or achieve a lower group grade. Good group work skills are the means with which to deal with such situations. It can help to:

- **identify the cause** (eg does someone have a good reason for not contributing?)
- **focus on the group, not the person** (eg *"We've got a problem, what can we do about it?"*)
- **focus on the problem, not the person** (eg not *"You are lazy"*, rather, *"If it isn't done we won't meet the deadline"*)
- **express your feelings before they get out of hand** (eg *"I am worried about ..."* ; *"I am getting angry about ..."*)

The chapters on "Negotiating and Assertiveness" may help here (see Contents).

21.5 YOUR INDIVIDUAL GROUP WORK SKILLS

21.5.1 Formal roles

In small cooperative groups, formal roles may not be necessary. In larger groups or where more structure is needed, it can help to have a chairperson and a secretary for meetings, or perhaps a co-ordinator for a project. These roles could be fixed or you could rotate them so that everybody can practise them. It is a good idea to encourage flexibility in group members.

A chairperson:

- agrees an agenda (asks for items from the group), either in advance or at the start of a meeting
- helps the group work through the agenda and keeps an eye on time
- encourages contributions, involves quiet people, asks talkative people to let others speak
- makes people feel comfortable.

A secretary:

- takes accurate notes (minutes) of meetings (it can be helpful to ask the chairperson to use the final five minutes to check what has been said and to clarify the actions to be taken)
- arranges meetings, venues.

A project group coordinator:

- is similar to a secretary, but may also keep track of who is doing what.

Does the group need a leader and, if so, what sort of leadership would be appropriate for the situation? If vital decisions need to be made quickly you may need a leader. In other situations – eg where gaining everybody's agreement and sharing responsibility are important – it may be better to operate collectively.

21.5.2 How you behave in groups

The following list, from Turner (1983), describes how people may behave in groups. You could use it to identify how you behaved in a particular group situation – eg a project group meeting.

Roles	Behaviour	Notes
task roles	<ul><li>initiates</li><li>seeks opinions</li><li>gives opinions</li><li>elaborates</li><li>coordinates</li><li>summarises</li></ul>	

Roles	Behaviour	Notes
maintenance roles	• encourages • gatekeeps (keeps the group to the task) • sets standards • expresses group feelings/reactions	
task and maintenance roles	• evaluates • diagnoses • tests for consensus/ agreement • mediates • compromises • relieves tension • makes jokes	

You could also use the following list, also from Turner (1983), to identify any of your behaviours which are unhelpful in a group.

✔

Unhelpful behaviour	
being overly aggressive	
blocking (rejecting ideas without due consideration, going off at tangents)	
self-confession	
competing	
seeking sympathy	
special pleading (for own concerns or interests)	
horsing around	
seeking recognition (excessive/loud talking, unsociable behaviour)	

21.5.3 Action planning

Are there aspects of your behaviour when in groups that you'd like to change? If so, you might wish to try out new behaviours. You could seek feedback from group members, tutors or workplace supervisors, where relevant, about:

- **how well you did your elements of the work**
- **how you behaved in the group**
- **how flexible you are when you operate in a group. Are you able to take on different roles or tasks if necessary?**

In completing the box overleaf you could consider sources of help, eg:

- **other chapters in this book**
- **books on group skills (see bibliography – libraries may have many more, including videos)**
- **friends (they may help you monitor what you are doing), and tutors**
- **a diary (you could keep a record of what you do).**

Return to Section 21.1. Has this SkillPack met your needs? If not, what else do you need to do? What further help do you need? From where or whom?

Please complete the box overleaf.

NOTES

What I do that is helpful

What I do that is unhelpful

What I would like to do differently

Actions I could take to change things in the future

NOTES

21.6 REFERENCES AND BIBLIOGRAPHY

Libraries may have materials on this skill area. The following give examples:

Johnson, D. W. and Johnson, F. P. (1991), *Joining Together: Group Theory and Group Skills*, Prentice Hall.

Rackham, N. and Morgan, T. (1977), *Behaviour Analysis in Training*, McGraw Hill.

Turner, C. (1983), *Developing Interpersonal Skills*, The Further Education Staff College.

22
NEGOTIATING AND ASSERTIVENESS

by Sue Drew and Rosie Bingham

CONTENTS

Our effectiveness in most situations depends, at least in part, on how well we deal with other people. What we and others want out of a situation is rarely identical and this usually means that we have to negotiate. This applies to:

• **day to day situations** – eg who does domestic jobs

• **your course** – eg group projects involve agreeing who does what; you may have to agree with a tutor work to carry out and then agree a grade or mark for it; you may need to get help from busy tutors or technicians

• **work placement or employment** – eg in all jobs you have to agree work activities with other people; in many jobs (surveying, social work, contract management, buying, selling etc) negotiation is a crucial element.

We suggest you use this SkillPack:

• **when you find yourself in a situation where you need to negotiate or be assertive**
• **on an ongoing basis to help you review and monitor what you do.**

When you have completed it you should be able to:

1 identify your own needs, goals, responsibilities and rights; check on others' understanding of your own position
2 clarify your own understanding of others' needs, goals, responsibilities and rights
3 know of strategies to use and their possible effects and anticipate their possible effects in a given situation
4 implement strategies in given situations and review their effectiveness in terms of meeting goals which are mutually acceptable
5 identify strengths and weaknesses of your own negotiating with others, and identify actions to build on strengths and improve weaknesses
6 monitor progress on actions identified, and review goals.

You should be able to use these elements of the skill on the course and in your personal and professional practice (eg placement). You should need little or no support from tutors and others.

NOTES

22.1 INTRODUCTION: A REVIEW OF THE BASICS

The following aspects are covered in the equivalent SkillPack in Part I. We suggest that you rate yourself against them on a scale where 1 = "very well" and 4 = "in need of considerable improvement".

✔

	1	2	3	4
I'm aware of how I currently try to agree matters with others.				
I am familiar with the following negotiating strategies: • separate the people from the problem • focus on interests not positions • generate options before deciding • agree criteria against which to judge solutions.				
I know what assertiveness is.				
I'm aware of when I am assertive, passive, manipulative or aggressive.				
I know why I don't behave assertively.				
I can identify my own needs and goals.				
I can identify other people's needs and goals				
I am familiar with assertiveness techniques: • "broken record" • acknowledging criticisms • accepting compliments • asking for clarification • avoiding preambles • acknowledging and recognising my own feelings • "going up the gears" • being aware of my personal appearance • saying "no" without excuses.				

If in doubt about any of these – refer to the equivalent SkillPack in Part I before reading on.

22.2 GOALS AND NEEDS

Throughout the remainder of this SkillPack we use the following situation as an example:

You want to ask a lecturer or a workplace supervisor for advice or help.

22.2.1 Know what you want

Firstly, be sure what you want or need. It can help to ask yourself the following questions before any meeting takes place. Knowing exactly what you want or need in advance will mean that you will be more coherent when you discuss the issue.

What is the basic issue or problem?

What are my feelings about this situation?

Do my feelings about the situation really relate to the other person(s) directly involved? (They might, or they might really be about other issues which are not directly related to them – eg a general high stress level, a general feeling of well-being or of dissatisfaction).

What do I want to happen?

What is my responsibility?

What is their responsibility?

What is somebody else's responsibility?

What rights do I have in this situation?

22.2.2 What do they want?

What are "the others" likely to want or need? What is good or difficult about the situation they are in? For example, a lecturer or workplace supervisor may:

* **want you to do well**
* **want to help but be unsure what help you need**
* **be very busy at work**
* **be worried about other personal problems of which you are unaware.**

Clearly you cannot accurately know what another person thinks, but what is your best guess? Can you put yourself in their position?

What is likely to be their basic issue or problem?

What are their feelings likely to be about this?

What information do they need in order to deal with the issue or problem?

What is rightly their responsibility?

What rights do they have in this situation?

22.2.3 Putting it together

Difficulties in finding mutually acceptable solutions often arise from misunderstanding. Are others clear about what you want? Are you clear about what they want?

* **Should you put all *your* cards on the table immediately? What effect would that have?**
* **Should you begin by asking the other person what they want or how they see things?**

The best approach depends on the situation. In whose advantage is it to begin?

One approach is to lay out the issue generally so that both parties are aware of the "agenda" (eg *"I need to talk to you about my workload"*). You could then ask the other person for their views (eg *"What do you think my priorities should be?"*) before stating what you want.

Whichever approach you use, check out whether everybody understands. Check also that others have understood you (eg *"Do you need any more information?"*) and that you have understood them (eg *"Did I understand you correctly that ...?"*).

22.3 GOOD COMMUNICATIONS

Effective communication means communicating in a way which helps you meet your goals. It is therefore difficult to apply general rules because what is effective depends on the situation and what all the parties want. For example, if your tutor is very busy when you call to see her/him, s/he may be less sympathetic than at another time. If your goal is to get help it may be counterproductive to insist on it there and then. It may be better to ask to discuss it at a more convenient time.

Being assertive involves saying what you need in a way which respects what the other person needs. It is different from being passive (*"I'm sorry I troubled you"*), manipulative (*"But if you don't see me now I know I'll fail"*) or aggressive (*"It's your job to see me now"*).

It might help to think of the approaches you could use in a situation which you currently face, in relation to the following questions:

- **Have you used similar approaches in the past?**
- **What effect would it have on you if you were on the receiving end?**
- **What short-term effect might it have on the other person?**
- **What long-term effect might it have on your relationship with the other person?**
- **Will it lead to a solution which is mutually acceptable?**

Evaluate your possible approaches in the box below.

Approach/strategy	Comments

22.4 YOUR ATTRIBUTES IN A NEGOTIATING SITUATION

22.4.1 Strengths

Which of your attributes are an advantage when attempting to agree matters with others? Identifying them can make you feel more confident. You need to beware, however, of using your strengths manipulatively – eg charm which is used to manipulate others can appear as "smarminess".

✔

Possible strengths
Humour
Relaxed manner
Trustworthy, reliable
Good listener
Ability to explain clearly
Patience
Others (please add your own):

22.4.2 "Weaknesses"

Which of your attributes might cause problems in negotiating with others? (eg possible "weaknesses" may include impatience, not listening, interrupting, being pushy, being tentative, being irritable, being very quiet etc)

What could you do to:

- **avoid them?**
- **change them?**
- **allow for them?**

"Weakness"	Actions to take

NOTES

22.5 ONGOING IMPROVEMENTS

You will constantly encounter situations where you need to negotiate and sometimes what you do will work and sometimes not. It is important to build on your experiences to become increasingly effective. You could keep a diary to record and review progress, or you could return to this SkillPack at regular intervals to do so.

Questions you could ask yourself include the following:

What works for me?

What doesn't work for me?

What are the effects of certain approaches or strategies?

Am I feeling any better about my dealings with others?

Are others reacting any more positively to me?

Are my needs/goals being met?

Having answered these questions, what do you need to improve?

Areas for improvement	Actions to take

22.6 REFERENCES AND BIBLIOGRAPHY

NOTES

Libraries may have materials on this skill area. The following give examples:

Dickson, A. (1982), *A Woman in Your Own Right*, Quartet Books.

Fisher, R. and Ury, W. (1987), *Getting to Yes. How to Negotiate to Agreement Without Giving In*, Arrow Books.

Moores, R. (1989), *Negotiating Skills*, Industrial Society.

Scott, B. and Billing, B. (1990), *Negotiating Skills in Engineering and Construction*, Thomas Telford.

Steele, P., Murphy, J. and Russill, R. (1989), *It's a Deal: A Practical Negotiation Handbook*, McGraw-Hill.

Townend, A. (1991), *Developing Assertiveness*, Routledge.

23
COPING WITH PRESSURE

by Sue Drew and Rosie Bingham

CONTENTS

This SkillPack aims to help you cope more effectively with those pressures which you can anticipate and those which you can't.

Developing the ability to cope with pressure makes you more likely to succeed on your course. Inevitably you will experience pressures – heavy course workload, applying for jobs and studying for exams, many social and other activities.

After you have graduated or gained your diploma, employment is likely to bring its own pressures, as may other areas of your life. Coping well with pressure means being more effective, healthier and able to enjoy what you do.

We suggest you use this SkillPack:

- **when you anticipate a pressurised time ahead (exams, for example)**
- **if you currently feel under pressure**
- **to handle ongoing pressures.**

When you have completed it, you should be able to:

1 identify, seeking feedback from others, your own reactions and usual responses to pressure and recognise signals of your own stress at an early stage
2 anticipate and identify possible sources of pressure at an early stage
3 monitor the effectiveness of your own reactions and responses, and identify needs for change
4 plan short-term goals and actions to allow for changing circumstances
5 identify at what point you need support and actively seek and use it
6 put plans into action, record and review progress in relation to changing circumstances.

You should be able to use this skill in any area of your life, with support from lecturers or tutors, university or college or outside support agencies.

23.1 INTRODUCTION: THE BASICS

Can you put into practice the basics of coping with pressure? You could score yourself on the following on a scale of 1-4, where 1 = "very well" and 4 = "needs considerable attention". You could use the margin for notes (eg on how you respond effectively or ineffectively to pressure).

✔

Basic information skills	1	2	3	4
I'm aware of what I tend to find pressurising.				
I'm able to identify current sources of pressure.				
I'm aware of how I respond to pressure in an effective/positive way.				
I'm aware of how I respond to pressure in a negative way.				
I'm aware of the advantages and disadvantages of how I respond to pressure.				
I'm able to use strategies to deal with pressure: • removing the cause of the pressure • trying new approaches • putting things into perspective • keeping fit • relaxation techniques • seeking feedback from others • seeking help.				

The equivalent SkillPack in Part I covers all the above items. Do your ratings suggest that you would find it useful to refer back to it?

23.2 RECOGNISING PRESSURE EARLY

Recognising pressure early, or even before it starts at all, can be very helpful. Pressure can creep up on you. Once you get to the point of feeling overwhelmed it is harder (though not impossible) to cope.

What one person considers pressurising, another might not. What sort of things do you usually tend to find pressurising (see box overleaf)?

How can you spot pressure early or anticipate it (see box overleaf)?

- **Although exactly the same situation may not recur, you could look out for situations similar to those you have found pressurising in the past –** eg being required to meet several deadlines close together; having to deal with certain sorts of people.
- **You could become more sensitive to your own positive and negative reactions to pressure. Consult the equivalent SkillPack in Part I.**
- **Stress can occur if you find it difficult to react positively or to use up the tension caused by pressure.** What are your early warning signs? For example, positives may include excitement and exhilaration; negatives may include not sleeping and irritability.

Are you experiencing any current pressures? Can you spot any pressures building up now or any which may occur in the near future? You need to maintain a balance between being prepared in a positive way and negatively expecting the worse.

Please use the boxes overleaf for your responses.

NOTES

Areas which I tend to find pressurising

My own early warning signs of stress

Current pressures	Pressures just beginning	Possible future pressures

23.3 UNANTICIPATED PRESSURES

In the past have you encountered pressures you hadn't anticipated? A sudden rush of work? An increase in demands placed on you? A crisis? What did you do? Was it effective or not?

What might have made things better? Here the focus should not be on factors outside yourself, over which you may have no control, but within yourself.

You might like to consider:

- **your goals (what were you trying to achieve?)**
- **your attitudes (were they helpful?)**
- **your feelings (were they justified?)**
- **your behaviour (did it meet your goals?).**

What I did	Effectiveness

Possible strategies for dealing with the unexpected include the following:

- **Don't plan your time so tightly** that an unanticipated pressure will become the straw that breaks the camel's back. Build in leeway (see the chapters on "Organising Yourself and Your Time", see Contents).
- **Be clear about what you currently want out of life.** Is the unexpected pressure worth your concern?
- **Say "no" to unreasonable sudden demands.** (See the chapters on "Negotiating and Assertiveness", see Contents).
- **Prioritise.** What else can be put aside or abandoned?
- **Stop, stand back, think it through, talk it over with somebody.**

What else have you done in the past that worked (or didn't)?

It is tempting to follow gut reactions when faced with the unexpected. What is likely to be the result? Positive? Negative? How could you either use "good" gut reactions to the full or stop "bad" ones for long enough to identify a more effective response?

23.4 PLANNING AHEAD

It might now help to draw up a plan for the short term (eg this week), the middle term (eg this month), the longer term (eg this semester, this year). It is important to build into each stage an allowance for the unexpected (even at a relatively simple level such as allowing longer for queues than you expect).

Things nearly always take longer than you think and if the unexpected doesn't materialise you'll have a bonus in terms of extra time and energy!

Short-term pressure	Middle-term pressure	Long-term pressure

Short-term plans	Middle-term plans	Long-term plans

If you find planning difficult refer to the chapters on "Organising Yourself and Your Time" (see Contents).

COPING WITH PRESSURE DEVELOPMENT 303

23.5 LOOKING AFTER YOURSELF

✔

Are you:	
doing things you enjoy as well as things you have to do?	
giving yourself treats?	
letting yourself off the hook, giving yourself a break?	
resting, relaxing, sleeping?	
having fun, pursuing interests?	
keeping fit?	
eating properly?	
not overdrinking alcohol?	
not oversmoking?	

Are you identifying at what point you need support and where you could get such support? This will vary from individual to individual. What is important is knowing what your "point" is and being unconcerned about whether other people's "points" occur sooner or later than yours.

For example:

Pressure	Possible point at which support is needed	Possible support
Gathering information for an assignment.	Have looked in library catalogues, CD-ROM but can't find material.	Library Information Desk.
Several coinciding deadlines.	Can't see how to meet them all.	Lecturers.
Health problem.	Recurring, persistent, interfering with effectiveness.	Medical Service.

You might find it helpful to fill in the same table in relation to your own circumstances.

Pressure	Possible point at which support is needed	Possible support

NOTES

It may be appropriate to talk things over with the same source of support at an early stage, or to ask for more support if you are feeling stressed.

For example a tutor might help in discussing how to plan your time, or give advice on a serious personal problem which is affecting you.

Possible sources of support include:

- **lecturers, tutors**
- **friends, other students, family members**
- **your university or college** – eg
  - Library
  - Computer Services
  - Careers Service
  - Counselling Service
  - Guidance Service
  - Medical Service
  - Chaplaincy
  - Recreation Services
  - Hall Wardens
  - Student Union
  - International Office
- **a local information service***
- **the Citizens' Advice Bureau***
- **Social Services**
- **Relate (supports pressure caused by relationship problems)***
- **your family doctor/GP.**

* The local telephone directory will have the contact numbers

This is only a short list to act as a stimulus for ideas. Any of the agencies listed above would themselves know of other individuals or groups who may be more relevant.

23.6 CHANGING THINGS

What can you do differently to improve your ability to cope with pressure? This is not a once-and-for-all question but one which needs to be repeated as circumstances change. The following can help you identify areas to change and then monitor and review those areas:

Areas needing attention	Actions I can take/sources of support	New circumstances	Progress/notes

NOTES

23.7 REFERENCES AND BIBLIOGRAPHY

Libraries may have materials on this skill area. The following give examples:

Atkinson, J. M. (1988), *Coping with Stress at Work*, Thorsons Publishers.

Cooper, C., Cooper, R. and Eaker, L. (1988), *Living with Stress*, Penguin Books.

Farmer, R., Monahan, L. and Hekeler, R. (1984), *Stress Management for Human Services*, Sage Publications.

Fontana, D. (1989), *Problems in Practice – Managing Stress*, The British Psychological Society and Routledge.

Looker, T. and Gregson, O. (1989), *Stresswise*, Hodder & Stoughton.

Patel, C. (1989), *The Complete Guide to Stress Management*, Optima.

24 REVISING AND EXAMINATION TECHNIQUES

by Sue Drew and Rosie Bingham

CONTENTS

This SkillPack aims to help you give your best performance and to cope effectively with the increasing demands of exams as you progress through your course.

Many courses use exams as a principal means of assessing students. Skills in this area may be vital to academic success. As you progress through your course, exams are likely to test more advanced abilities and draw on a wider range of material. You can improve your performance by identifying techniques which could work well for you.

Practising these revision and examination techniques during your course should improve your performance in final exams.

This SkillPack assumes you have identified what you need to revise and are familiar with basic revision techniques. If this is not the case, refer to the equivalent SkillPack in Part I "Revising and Examination Techniques".

We suggest you use this SkillPack:

- **in relation to an exam or set of exams you have to take**
- **to help you plan your revision well in advance of those exams (we suggest you read in advance through both the sections on revision (Sections 24.2, 24.3, 24.4) and exam techniques (Sections 24.5, 24.6, 24.7), as your response to the exam technique section may cause you to change your revision).**

When you have completed this SkillPack, you should be able to:

1 identify the purpose and format of the exam, and what examiners are seeking (including external examiners)
2 identify and prioritise which material to revise
3 identify which revision techniques used to date are best suited to yourself, the material and the format of the exam
4 plan actions and time for revision within given constraints, allowing for your own strengths and weaknesses
5 monitor progress, review original goals and amend plans accordingly
6 identify your own usual responses to the examination situation and plan strategies to improve performance
7 identify what the question means and analyse what is required
8 identify which questions to answer in an order which will maximise performance
9 plan answers to include appropriate evidence evaluation and criticism of that evidence
10 review your own revision and exam strategies and identify improved methods for the future.

You should be able to use the above elements of the skill on your course and in further professional exams, with little or no support.

NOTES

24.1 YOUR CURRENT REVISION AND EXAM TECHNIQUES

Do you use the following techniques in revising?　　　　　　　　✔

Identifying in advance the format of the exam and what it is for.	
Finding out what the examiners want.	
Identifying which revision techniques seem appropriate for the subject, the exam and yourself, eg: • sorting your material out, checking you understand it • identifying questions likely to arise • relating topics to each other • making summaries and 'flash cards' • making lists • making and listening to tape recordings of material • testing yourself, or a friend • allowing for your own capacity for concentration • working in a pleasant environment.	
Making a revision plan.	
Monitoring your revision progress and amending your plan.	
Identifying what you need to improve next time round.	

Do you use the following techniques in exams?　　　　　　　　✔

Spending the first 10 minutes: • clarifying the instructions • identifying what the questions mean and what is required • deciding which questions to answer in what order • planning how much time to allocate to the questions.	
Planning answers.	
Using appropriate evidence for your statements.	
Presenting your information neatly.	
Doing a final check on your work.	
Identifying what you need to improve next time round.	

If you are unable to tick many of these revision and examination techniques, it may help to refer to the equivalent SkillPack in Part I, which considers all the above basics. This SkillPack considers how you can improve on these.

24.2 WHAT EXAMINERS WANT

To perform well in exams it is important to know what is expected. Misunderstanding about this can lead to poor results. For example, a student may think that an exam answer requires much detailed factual information without any evaluation of it. If the examiner is actually looking for an evaluation, the student will receive a low mark and be puzzled about the reason for this.

As you progress through your course you should find that the things looked for by examiners change in the following ways:

- **When you first start on a course a subject may be new to you and lecturers allow for this. By the end of the course they will expect deeper knowledge and understanding of a subject.**
- **Examiners are likely to become more concerned that you can analyse and criticise information – that you can look at "why", what opposing views there are, what are the shortcomings of certain arguments, what is inaccurate.**
- **They may want you to bring a variety of information, or elements of a problem, or aspects of a theory together to identify essential points.**
- **They may also look for an understanding of the whole field and how a topic fits into it. They are likely to want you to demonstrate "deep learning" – ie an understanding of concepts and principles – as well as "surface learning" – ie memorising facts.**
- **They may want you to demonstrate what you know, rather than find out what you don't know. In the early stages of courses, assessment aims to identify shortcomings so that you can improve on them. Final exams can be seen more as a summary of what you know.**
- **There may be a shift away from merely reproducing what you know towards being able to apply that knowledge. You might find that, in first-year exams, the question gives you hints about how to answer it, but that by the final year questions are worded with fewer hints.**

In order to find out what is needed you could:

- **look at past exam papers**
- **look at the aims of the course or programme you are taking**
- **ask your lecturers**
- **read the exam regulations.** They will tell you: what you need to do to pass; what happens if you fail; what evidence you need if you are ill before or during the exam or have serious personal problems likely to affect your performance.

In some cases you might also need to consider what an external examiner might look for. Courses have an external examiner – usually a lecturer from another university or college – who ensures that procedures are followed and standards maintained. Your lecturers can tell you how the external examiner will be involved.

Having investigated what you think will be wanted in your exam(s), it may be helpful to summarise your conclusions and to check them out with your lecturers. You can keep referring back to this as you prepare for the exam.

If you have a disability which may influence your exam performance discuss alternative arrangements with your lecturer well in advance.

If you are ill or have any other difficulties which have affected your revision or exam performance, you may be able to ask the examiners to make allowances for these "mitigating circumstances".

You will usually need to present your case in a certain way and to provide evidence (eg doctor's notes), so ask your lecturers as soon as possible what counts as a "mitigating circumstance", what the procedure is and what evidence is needed.

NOTES

What will the examiner(s) be looking for in the exams you will be sitting?

24.3 PRIORITISING WHAT TO REVISE

This SkillPack assumes you have identified what you need to revise (if in doubt refer back to the equivalent SkillPack in Part I). Once you know what to revise you should prioritise the items. As you may have an increasing amount of material to cover, prioritising will help you maximise your marks by focusing your attention on the important areas.

In prioritising, consider the following questions:

How much time is available for revision?

How much material is there to cover?

What is the examiner looking for (see Section 24.2)?

What topics might you do best at?

What topics might you do worst at?

What topics are the crucial ones for the subject?

What do you like/dislike doing?

What other demands on your time will there be?

Others (make a list)

NOTES

What can you do if you encounter problems? For example, what happens if a crucial area which is very likely to crop up is the one you find most difficult?

What if you have other demands on your time or other personal difficulties?

What are your problems?

What are your options (generate as many ideas as possible)?

Who can help?

24.4 PLANNING REVISION

24.4.1 What revision techniques work for you?

This SkillPack assumes that you are familiar with basic revision techniques, such as those listed in Section 24.1. If this is not the case refer to the equivalent SkillPack in Part I. Which techniques suit you best? What are your strengths and weaknesses in revising? What does your experience to date tell you works best for you?

My strengths in revising – what I do	My weaknesses – what I do less well

Now go back over the above list. In the second column, which lists your "weaknesses", place a tick next to those you cannot avoid and must improve on. What do you need to do to improve?

NOTES

NOTES

24.4.2 Revision plan

Before you draw up a revision plan, we suggest you read Sections 24.5 and 24.6, which may give additional ideas for what to include. We also suggest you make a few photocopies of this blank plan. Review it at regular intervals, by asking yourself the following questions, then draw up a new plan using one of the blank sheets.

- **Are your priorities still the same?**
- **Is your timescale realistic? Have any unforeseen demands arisen?**
- **Are your revision techniques working?**

What to revise in priority order	By when? (deadlines)	What techniques will you use to revise?

24.5 THE EXAM ITSELF – YOUR REACTIONS

24.5.1 What do you usually do in exams?

By now you should have experience of taking exams at university or college. What do you usually do? Does it work? Is there anything you used to do in exams which no longer works? How do you feel in exams? What do they do to you? What do you need to do differently?

Positives	Negatives	Improvement needed

In considering how to improve, you could identify sources of help:

- **Share ideas with friends.**
- **Seek lecturers' advice.**
- **Look in libraries for materials on this topic.**
- **Look for courses on study skills.**
- **Consider for yourself what would help you. Sometimes identifying a problem makes the solution obvious.**

24.5.2 Coping with nerves

If you feel that your nervousness may hamper rather than improve your performance, you could consider past situations. What effect did nerves have? What might have made it better? Although solutions will vary from person to person, possibilities include:

- **Good preparation:** eg learning your topic well in advance, practising answering similar exam papers.
- **Finding out in advance what the exam conditions will be:** eg date, time, room, what the "rules" are (eg about going to the toilet/leaving early), what equipment you can take in. Going into an exam without being fully informed about its operation may increase anxiety.
- **Working out what to do in the first 10 minutes in what order and trying to keep to it:** (eg checking instructions, writing name, reading through the paper etc). Doing simple things first will calm you down. Jumping straight into a question without this planning/settling phase may cause you to misunderstand what has to be done and panic.
- **Making yourself as comfortable as possible for the exam:** have enough handkerchiefs, wear comfortable clothes (how hot/cold will it be?).
- **Taking care what do you do before an exam:** try to avoid drinking alcohol (exams and hangovers don't mix); being overtired (is it really worth staying up late to cram in extras?); take some exercise (walk to the exam).
- **Avoiding last-minute revision:** anxiety created by last-minute "surface learning" (ie memorising facts) may block out "deep learning" (ie understanding of principles and concepts), which is likely to be very important, particularly in final-year exams.

Work out in advance what you will do if you panic. Options include the following:

- **Stop,** close your eyes and breathe in to a count of six and out to a count of six, 10 times.
- **Stop,** reread the question and jot down in pencil any ideas you have, then sort them into some sort of order.
- **Stop,** and move on to another question, returning to the question with which you are having difficulty later.
- **Stop,** and do a question you **can** answer to get a "success" under your belt.

Whichever option you try, all involve **stopping what you are doing**, and then deciding what to do next.

24.6 GETTING THE BEST MARKS POSSIBLE

Basic techniques in dealing with exams are as follows:

- **Spend the first 10 minutes clarifying the instructions, what the questions mean, which you will answer, how long you will allocate to each, and in what order you will answer them.**
- **Watch the time and try to stick to your plan.**
- **Spend 10 minutes at the end checking your work.**

How can you improve your marks? What will get good marks in this sort of exam in your subject? If in doubt, check with your lecturer.

✔

Will accuracy be very important – eg dates, calculations, names?	
Will your writing style be important – eg spelling, grammar, how you express yourself?	
Will your presentation of data, visuals or your writing be important?	
Will they want to see each step of an argument or calculation or process?	
Will you be required to analyse information – eg what are the implications, underlying issues, correlations?	
Will you be required to be critical – eg considering questions like why, for whom, when, what are the alternatives, what are the shortcomings or inaccuracies?	
Will you need to back up your views, opinions, ideas with referenced evidence?	
Will how you argue your case be important?	
Will how well you organise the information included in your answer be important?	

The following subsections offer suggestions for improving on the basic exam techniques.

24.6.1 Practising in advance

You could identify a question you think will arise in your exam and draft a reply. Now look back at the items you ticked on the checklist above. Has your reply catered for those items?

You could do this exercise with a friend. Exchange questions and replies and look at each other's replies in the light of the ticked items. This should reveal where you need to improve. You may find that you need to be more critical or select more carefully the main points to cover, or be more accurate. You can then practise improving that area.

NOTES

24.6.2 Planning

Would it be best to answer those questions where you feel you will get high marks first, or to dispose of the more difficult ones? If you choose the latter option, make sure you leave enough time to do yourself justice on your best topics.

Do you operate best if you draft a brief outline answer before writing or if you write an answer straight off? If it is the latter, you will need to allow time for checking.

Are there any personal aspects you need to take into account – eg nervousness or a disability? How can you plan to deal with it? Will you need any special equipment? In the case of disability you may need to discuss this well in advance with your lecturer.

24.6.3 Dealing with different types of exams

Unseen exams

An unseen exam is one where you do not know in advance what the questions will be and you cannot take material in with you – eg essay- or problem-based papers; multiple choice (you choose one from several possible answers); short questions requiring short answers.

You may find that, as you progress through your course, you will encounter fewer multiple choice or short-answer exams, and more "seen exams". Do not assume that second-, third- or fourth-year exams will have the same format as first-year exams.

Seen exams

In seen exams you see part or all of the exam in advance – eg open book exams (where you can take source materials in with you); exams where you are given in advance a case study or data on which the exam will be based; exams where you take the question away and answer it in your own time rather than under exam conditions.

How can you deal effectively with seen exams?

One issue in seen exams is how much time you spend in preparation. There are two dangers – spending too little time because you feel you don't need to as you will have the material with you, or spending too much time. The latter may mean neglecting other subjects, and becoming bogged down.

In deciding how much time to spend, it might help to ask the following:

- **What proportion of the overall grade does the work represent?**
- **Are you likely to improve your overall grade by concentrating on this?**
- **How much work can you cope with before you feel stressed?**

A case study/data seen in advance

If you are given a case study or data in advance, you will need to make yourself very familiar with the material and look at it from all angles to see what issues might arise in the exam.

You may be allowed to take notes into the exam. If so, consider what notes would be most helpful – pulling out critical aspects from a case/data; notes on relevant theories; issues you think will crop up in the exam question.

Your notes must be easy to follow. Minutely written notes may be hard to decipher in the exam, especially if you are nervous. Headings, underlinings, marker pens, lists, diagrams may help.

Open book

In open book exams you should decide in advance whether to use the original material during the exam or to use notes summarising it. You also need some method of finding the correct sections in the material during the exam. You might feel flustered, so you will need a simple system.

Beware of overquoting from material. Whilst relevant quotes are important the examiner will want to see what your ideas/views/arguments are rather than read long rewritten extracts from the original.

Take away

Where the exam consists of a question you take away and answer in your own time, word limits may be given and you should stick to them.

Don't forget to allow time to write up; it may take longer than you anticipate.

Plagiarism

Avoid plagiarism. Plagiarism is where you copy somebody else's work without acknowledging it with a reference. It will be seen as cheating and may have serious consequences.

24.6.4 Organising material/ordering your answer

For exams taken under normal exam conditions, how much can you cover in the time allowed for the question? How much can you physically write, say, in the 30-45 minutes you have? 500 words?

If the average paragraph is 100 words, and if you make one main point per paragraph, you can make five main points. Which of the points you could make are the most important?

As your course progesses, exams are more likely to require you to organise information in a more effective way. Possibilities include:

- **a clear opening paragraph explaining what you intend to cover or what stance you are adopting; making your points clearly and in a clear order; having a final paragraph drawing conclusions and summarising**
- **a step-by-step procedure, where a sequence or stages are important**
- **a main initial point to make an impact which you then develop**
- **a series of points leading to a conclusion which has impact**
- **different sides of an argument**
- **theories or concepts together, though grouped by a theme**
- **an introduction; presentation of information; critique or evaluation; conclusions.**

24.6.5 Presentation of material

Headings, subheadings and a good layout make it easier to read and follow what you have written.

Any tables or graphs need to be clear with the correct labelling.

24.6.6 The final check

If you leave 10 minutes at the end of the exam to check your work, how can you best use that time? You might:

- **check a weak spot – eg a particular answer or something running through all answers (eg poor spelling)**
- **check on the layout – eg underlining headings, subheadings**
- **finish off a question**
- **check details, such as figures, references, names, dates.**

What will most improve your marks (see the checklist in Section 24.6)

24.6.7 Maximising your marks – ideas to try

Which of the ideas in Section 24.6 will you try?

24.7 IMPROVING YOUR PERFORMANCE

You may have further exams on your current course, or you may have exams in the future – for example for professional qualifications.

How could you improve your performance?

Revision		
Positives to build on	**Action**	**By (deadline)**
Areas to improve	**Action**	**By (deadline)**

Exams		
Positives to build on	**Action**	**By (deadline)**
Areas to improve	**Action**	**By (deadline)**

24.8 REFERENCES AND BIBLIOGRAPHY

Libraries may have materials on this skill. The following give examples:

Books and written material

Acres, D. (1992), *How to Pass Exams Without Anxiety*, How To Books.

Buzan, T. (1973), *Use Your Head*, BBC Publications.

Coles, M. and White, C. (1992), *How to Study and Pass Exams*, Collins.

Gibbs, G. (1981), *Teaching Students to Learn*, Open University Press.

Habeshaw, S., Habeshaw, J. and Gibbs, G. (1987), *53 Interesting Ways of Helping Your Students to Study*, Technical and Educational Services Limited.

Jacques, D. (1990), *Studying at the Polytechnic*, Education Methods Unit, Oxford Polytechnic.

National Extension College (1994), *Learning Skills*, Units 42-50 National Extension College.

Northedge, A. (1990), *The Good Study Guide*, Open University Press.

Videos

Secrets of Study (interactive video), Mast Learning Systems, 1989.

APPENDICES

REFERENCES AND BIBLIOGRAPHY

Chapter 1: How to Use this Book

Abson, D. (1984), "The effects of peer evaluation on the behaviour of undergraduate students working in tutorless groups" in Foot, H.C., Howe, C.J., Anderson, A., Tolmie, A.K. and Warden D.A. (eds), *Group and Interactive Learning*, Computational Mechanic's Publications.

Association of Graduate Recruiters (1993), *Roles for Graduates in the 21st Century, Getting the Balance Right*, AGR.

Becker, H.S., Beer, B. and Hughes, E. (1968), *Making the Grade. The Academic Side of College*, John Wiley.

Business and Technical Education Council (1992), *Common Skills and Core Themes. General Guidelines*, BTEC.

Confederation of British Industry (1989), *Towards a Skills Revolution*, CBI.

Council for National Academic Awards (1989), *CNAA Handbook*, CNAA.

Department of Education and Science (1985), *Better Schools*, Cmnd 9469, HMSO.

Department of Education and Science (1985), *The Development of Higher Education into the 1990s*, Cmnd 9524, HMSO.

Department of Education and Science (1986), *Working Together – Education and Training*, Cmnd 9823, HMSO.

Department of Education and Science (1987), *Higher Education – Meeting the Challenge*, Cmnd 114, HMSO.

Kolb, D.A. (1984), *Experiential Learning*, Prentice Hall.

Manpower Services Commission (1981), *A New Training Initiative. A Consultative Document*, MSC.

Marton, F. and Saljo, R. (1984), "Approaches to learning" in Marton, F., Hounsell, D. and Entwhistle, N., *The Experience of Learning*, Scottish Academic Press.

National Advisory Body (1986), *Transferable Skills in Employment - The Contribution of Higher Education*, NAB.

National Curriculum Council (1990), *Core Skills 16–19*, NCC.

Oates, T. (1992a), "Core Skills and transfer: aiming high", *Educational and Training International*, **29** (3), pp.227–39.

Oates, T. (1992b), *Developing and Piloting the NCVQ Core Skill Units. An Outline of Methods and a Summary of Findings*, NCVQ.

Schon, D.A. (1987), *Educating the Reflective Practitioner*, Jossey Bass.

Trades Union Congress (1989), *Skills 2000*, TUC.

Chapters 2 and 14: Identifying Strengths and Improving Skills

AGCAS (1992), *Where Next? Exploring your Future*, (a series of booklets) AGCAS.

Booklet 1   "Taking the plunge"

Booklet 2   "Reflections"

Booklet 3   "Sharpening the image"

NOTES

Booklet 4   "Choices"

AGCAS (1992) *Discovering Yourself. A Self-assessment Guide for Older Students*, AGCAS.

Chapters 3 and 15: Organising Yourself and Your Time

Buzan, T. (1973), *Use your Head*, BBC Publications.

Hopson, B. and Scally, M. (1989), *Time Management: Conquer the Clock*, Lifeskills.

Jacques, D. (1990), *Studying at the Polytechnic*, Educational Methods Unit, Oxford Polytechnic.

Northedge, A. (1990), *The Good Study Guide*, Open University Press.

Stuart, R. R. (1989), *Managing Time*, The Pegasus Programme Understanding Industry Inst.

Chapter 4: Note Taking

Buzan, T. (1973), *Use your Head*, BBC Publications.

Gibbs, G. (1981), *Teaching Students to Learn*, Open University Press.

Habeshaw, S., Habeshaw, J. and Gibbs, G. (1987), *53 Interesting Ways of Helping your Students to Study*, Technical & Educational Services Ltd.

Jacques, D. (1990), *Studying at the Polytechnic*, Educational Methods Unit, Oxford Polytechnic.

National Extension College (1994), *Learning Skills Resource Bank: Notes for Tutors and Trainers*, NEC.

Northedge, A. (1990), *The Good Study Guide*, Open University Press.

Stuart, R. R. (1989), *Managing Time*, The Pegasus Programme Understanding Industry Inst.

Chapters 5 and 16: Gathering and Using Information

Bell, J. (1987), *Doing Your Own Research Project: A Guide for First-time Researchers in Education and Social Science*, Open University Press.

Cohen, L. and Manion, L. (1985 edn), *Research Methods in Education*, Croom Helm.

Deer Richardson, L. (1992), *Techniques of Investigation: An Introduction to Research Methods*, National Extension College.

Huff, D. (1973), *How to Lie with Statistics*, Penguin Books.

Northedge, A. (1990), *The Good Study Guide*, Open University Press.

Pauk, W. (1989), *How to Study in College*, (4th edn), Houghton Mifflin.

Reynolds J. E. F. (ed.) (1993), *Martindale the Extra Pharmacopoeia*, The London Pharmaceutical Press.

Secrets of Study (interactive video) (1989), Mast Learning Systems.

Chapters 6 and 17: Essay Writing

Allen, R. E. (1986) *The Oxford Spelling Dictionary*, Oxford University Press.

Brown, S., Rust, C. and Gibbs, G. (1994), *Strategies for Diversifying Assessment*, Oxford Centre for Staff Development.

Burnard, P. (1989), "Experiential learning and androgogy – negotiated learning in nurse education: a critical appraisal", *Nurse Education Today*, **9** (5), pp.300–306.

Cederblom, J. and Paulsen, P. W. (1990), *Critical Reasoning*, (3rd edn), Wadsworth.

Clancy, J. and Ballard, B. (1992), *How to Write Essays. A Practical Guide for Students*, Longman.

Collinson, D., Kirkup, G., Kyd R., and Slocombe, L. (1992), *Plain English* (2nd edn) Oxford University Press.

Fairbairn, G. J. and Winch, C. (1991), *Reading, Writing and Reasoning: A Guide for Students*, Society for Research into Higher Education and Oxford University Press.

Hallam, J. and Marshment, M. (1995), "Training experience: case studies in the reception of 'Oranges are Not the Only Fruit'", *Screen*, **36** (1), pp.1–16.

Hamp-Lyons, L. and Heasley, B. (1987), *Study Writing. A Course in Written English for Academic and Professional Purposes*, Cambridge University Press.

Hounsell, D. and Murray, R. (1992), "Essay writing for active learning"; *Effective Learning and Teaching in Higher Education*, CVCP Universities Staff Development and Training Unit.

Jones, S. (1993), *The Language of the Genes*, Flamingo.

Murphy, R. (1994), *English Grammar in Use* (2nd edn.) A self-study reference and practice book for intermediate students, Cambridge University Press.

Murray, D. (1982), "Learning by teaching", *Selected Articles on Writing and Teaching*, Heinemann.

Newby, M. (1989), *Writing. A Guide for Students*, Cambridge University Press.

Pearson, R. A. and Phelps, T. (1993), *Academic Vocabulary and Argument*, PAVIC Publications.

Raichura, L. (1987), "Learning by doing", *Nursing Times*, **83** (13), pp.59–61.

Romaine, S. (1989), *Bilingualism*, Basil Blackwell.

Thorn, L. (1995), "Using outreach in a rural tertiary college", *Adults Learning* **6** (8), pp.243–6.

Watney, S. (1991), "Aids: the second decade: risk research and modernity", Aggleton, P., Hart, P. and Davies, P. (eds), *Aids Responses, Interventions and Care*, Falmer Press.

Young, A. (1995), "Peer and parental pressure within the sociolinguistic environment: an Anglo-French comparative study of teenage foreign language learners", *Language in a Changing Europe*, BAAL.

Chapters 7 and 18: Report Writing

Bell, J. (1987), *Doing your Research Project: A Guide for First-time Researchers in Education and Social Science*, Open University Press.

Cooper, B. M. (1964), *Writing Technical Reports*, Penguin Books.

Gowers, E. (1986), *The Complete Plain Words*, HMSO.

Huff, D. (1973), *How to Lie with Statistics*, Penguin Books.

Peel, M. (1990), *Improving Your Communication Skills*, Kogan Page.

Stanton, N. (1990), *Communication*, Macmillan Education.

Chapters 8 and 19: Oral Presentation

Bernstein, D. (1988), *Put It Together. Put It Across. The Craft of Business Presentation*, Cassell.

Discovering Presentations, (interactive video) – Longmans Training: British Telecom 1991.

Peel, M. (1990), *Improving your Communication Skills*, Kogan Page.

Peel, M. (1992), *Successful Presentation in a Week*, Hodder & Stoughton.

Stanton, N. (1990), *Communication*, Macmillan Education.

The Floor is Yours Now – A Guide to Successful Presentations Gower, (24 minutes).

We Can't Hear You at The Back (part of a series – Work is a Four-letter Word) BBC, 1992 (30 minutes).

Chapters 9 and 20: Solving Problems

Comino Foundation (1994), GRASP® – *Getting Results and Solving Problems*, Comino

NOTES

Foundation, 29 Holloway Lane, Amersham, HP6 6DJ.

Cowan, J. (nd), *Individual Approaches to Problem Solving*, Department of Civil Engineering, Heriot Watt University.

de Bono, E. (1982), *De Bono's Thinking Course*, Ariel Books, BBC.

Chapters 10 and 21: Group Work

Johnson, D. W. and Johnson, F. P. (1991), *Joining Together: Group Theory and Group Skills*, Prentice Hall.

Rackham, N. and Morgan, T. (1977), *Behaviour Analysis in Training*, McGraw Hill.

Turner, C. (1983), *Developing Interpersonal Skills*, The Further Education Staff College.

Chapters 11 and 22: Negotiating and Assertiveness

Berne, E. (1981) *Games People Play: The Psychology of Human Relationships*, Castle.

Dickson, A. (1982), *A Woman in Your Own Right*, Quartet Books.

Fisher, R. and Ury, W. (1987), *Getting to Yes. How to Negotiate to Agreement Without Giving In*, Arrow Books.

Moores, R. (1989), *Negotiating Skills*, Industrial Society.

Scott, B. and Billing, B. (1990), *Negotiating Skills in Engineering and Construction*, Thomas Telford.

Steele, P., Murphy, J., and Russill, R. (1989), *It's a Deal: A Practical Negotiation Handbook*, McGraw-Hill.

Townend, A. (1991), *Developing Assertiveness*, Routledge.

Chapters 12 and 23: Coping with Pressure

Atkinson, J. M. (1988), *Coping with Stress at Work*, Thorsons Publishers.

Cooper, C., Cooper, R. and Eaker, L. (1988), *Living with Stress*, Penguin Books

Farmer, R., Monahan, L. and Hekeler, R. (1984), *Stress Management for Human Services*, Sage Publications.

Fontana, D. (1989), *Problems in Practice - Managing Stress*, The British Psychological Society and Routledge.

Looker, T. and Gregson, O. (1989), *Stresswise*, Hodder & Stoughton.

Patel, C. (1989), *The Complete Guide to Stress Management*, Optima.

Chapters 13 and 24: Revising and Examination Techniques

Acres, D. (1982), *How to Pass Exams Without Anxiety*, How To Books, Hamlyn.

Buzan, T. (1973), *Use Your Head*, BBC Publications.

Coles, M. and White, C. (1992), *How to Study and Pass Exams*, Collins.

Gibbs, G. (1981), *Teaching Students to Learn*, Open University Press.

Habeshaw, S., Habeshaw, J. and Gibbs, G. (1987), *53 Interesting Ways of Helping Your Students to Study*, Technical and Educational Services Limited.

Jacques, D. (1990), *Studying at the Polytechnic*, Education Methods Unit, Oxford Polytechnic.

National Extension College (1994), *Learning Skills*, Units 42-50 National Extension College.

Northedge, A. (1990) *The Good Study Guide*, Open University Press.

Secrets of Study (Interactive video), Mast Learning Systems, 1989.

STUDENT SKILLS PRODUCT LIST

The Student Skills Guide

A standard size paperback containing the text of all 23 SkillPacks laid out as a workbook. Students can either work through each chapter at Starter Level and then Development Level or select only the chapter relevant to their current activity. There is an introductory section explaining how to use the book and a bibliography.

This book is designed as a textbook and is available as an inspection copy for adoption consideration.

Paperback   350 pages   0 566 07847 3

Student Skills Tutor's Handbook

This large format paperback contains the text of all the SkillPacks (but not the right to photocopy them), together with an introductory section on how and when to use the SkillPacks to best effect. A special feature of the Tutor's Handbook is a listing of the Learning Outcomes for all 23 packs. A consolidated bibliography is also provided.

This book can be supplied on approval.

A4 Paperback 350 pages   0 566 07846 5

Student Skills SkillPack Masters

Lecturers purchasing a SkillPack Masters pack receive a set of photocopiable masters for both the Starter Level SkillPack and the Development Level SkillPack in the chosen subject. Also included is a Licence - valid for one year - to make up to 500 copies of each SkillPack for use within the Department purchasing the Masters. Each pack also comes with a SkillPack Guide giving details of how to use the SkillPacks to best effect and containing details of the Learning Outcomes of all the SkillPacks and a consolidated bibliography.

These SkillPack Masters cannot be supplied on approval.

ISBN	Title
0 566 07848 1	**Identifying Strengths and Improving Skills SkillPack Masters**
0 566 07849 X	**Organising Yourself and Your Time SkillPack Masters**
0 566 07850 3	**Note Taking SkillPack Masters***
0 566 07851 1	**Gathering and Using Information SkillPack Masters**
0 566 07852 X	**Essay Writing SkillPack Masters**
0 566 07853 8	**Report Writing SkillPack Masters**
0 566 07854 6	**Oral Presentation SkillPack Masters**
0 566 07855 4	**Solving Problems SkillPack Masters**
0 566 07856 2	**Group Work SkillPack Masters**
0 566 07857 0	**Negotiating and Assertiveness SkillPack Masters**
0 566 07858 9	**Coping with Pressure SkillPack Masters**
0 566 07859 7	**Revising and Examination Techniques SkillPack Masters**

A licence is available for all 23 SkillPacks at a reduced price.
* There is no Development Level SkillPack for Note Taking.

Student Skills SkillPacks

SkillPacks are available for distribution to students and are provided as A4 booklets shrinkwrapped in sets of ten. Starter Packs and Development Packs are available separately. A SkillPack Guide is also supplied with each order. The SkillPack Guide explains how to use the SkillPacks to best effect and also contains a consolidated bibliography and details of the Learning Outcomes for all 23 SkillPacks. Individual SkillPacks vary in length from 8 pages to 24 pages.

Whilst the SkillPacks cannot be supplied on approval, the Student Skills Tutor's Handbook demonstrates the full scope and approach of these materials. The price of the Handbook can also be redeemed against the cost of your first order for other SkillPack material.

ISBN	Title
Starter Level SkillPacks	
0 566 07871 6	**Identifying Strengths and Improving Skills**
0 566 07872 4	**Organising Yourself and Your Time**
0 566 07873 2	**Note Taking**
0 566 07874 0	**Gathering and Using Information**
0 566 07875 9	**Essay Writing**
0 566 07876 7	**Report Writing**
0 566 07877 5	**Oral Presentation**
0 566 07878 3	**Solving Problems**
0 566 07879 1	**Group Work**
0 566 07880 5	**Negotiating and Assertiveness**
0 566 07881 3	**Coping with Pressure**
0 566 07882 1	**Revising and Examination Techniques**
Development Level SkillPacks	
0 566 07860 0	**Identifying Strengths and Improving Skills**
0 566 07861 9	**Organising Yourself and Your Time**
0 566 07862 7	**Gathering and Using Information**
0 566 07863 5	**Essay Writing**
0 566 07864 3	**Report Writing**
0 566 07865 1	**Oral Presentation**
0 566 07866 X	**Solving Problems**
0 566 07867 8	**Group Work**
0 566 07868 6	**Negotiating and Assertiveness**
0 566 07869 4	**Coping with Pressure**
0 566 07870 8	**Revising and Examination Techniques**